TRADITIONAL NATURAL LAW AS THE SOURCE OF WESTERN
CONSTITUTIONAL LAW, PARTICULARLY IN THE UNITED STATES

TRADITIONAL NATURAL LAW AS THE SOURCE OF WESTERN CONSTITUTIONAL LAW, PARTICULARLY IN THE UNITED STATES

By Dante Figueroa

Adjunct Professor at the Georgetown Law Center and the
American University Washington College of Law

EDITORIAL JURÍDICA VENEZOLANA INTERNATIONAL

2 0 1 4

Depósito Legal: lf54020143402983
ISBN: 978-980-365-270-8

Edited by Editorial Jurídica Venezolana
Avda. Francisco Solano López, Torre Oasis, P.B., Local 4, Sabana Grande,
Apartado 17.598 - Caracas, 1015, Venezuela
Teléfono (058) (02) 762-25-53 / 762-38-42/ Fax. (058) (02) 763-52-39
Email: fejv@cantv.net
http://www.editorialjuridicavenezolana.com.ve

Printed by Ligthning Source, an Ingram Content company
Distributed by: Editorial Jurídica Venezolana International Inc.
Panamá, República de Panamá.
Email: editorialjuridicainternational@gmail.com

Formatting, Composition and Editing by: Mirna Pinto de Naranjo
Letter: Times New Roman, 10.5. Line Spacing: 11.
Text: 18 x 11.5. Dimension book: 22.9 x 15.2
Cover: Antonio Rosmini-Serbati (1797-1855), Italian Roman Catholic priest
and philosopher.

Saint Thomas Aquinas (1225-1274) Italian Dominican friar and priest

Το Σοφία [Wisdom]:
the ancient quest in the human comedy

AUTHOR'S NOTE

The author wishes to express his gratitude to professors Robert Barker, from the Duquesne University School of Law in Pittsburgh; Richard Stith, from the Valparaiso University School of Law in Indiana, and Dr. D.Q. McInerny, from Our Lady of Guadalupe Seminar, in Nebraska for their valuable comments during the preparation of this book. The author's gratitude goes also to Stephenie Reimer for her diligent editorial work, and to Chiara Vitiello for the translation of this manuscript into Italian. Unless otherwise specified, all translations are by the author.

His publications are available at http://ssrn.com/author=1015723, and he can be reached at df257@georgetown.edu

CONTENTS

CHAPTER VII:

CHAPTER VIII:

CHAPTER IX:

FOREWORD

Allan R. Brewer-Carías
Emeritus Professor, Central University of Venezuela

The author of this book, Professor Dante Figueroa, is a prominent lawyer, professor, and scholar of law, with an extensive library of published work discussed in diverse international settings. His work is distinguished by strong academic and vocational training, as well as extensive professional practice as a legal consultant in Chile and the United States.

He is not simply a theorist or philosopher of law, whose mastery is evidenced in his study on the influence of natural law in the formation of constitutional law in the Western world, but rather he is a renowned jurist, who with his legal practice, has successfully combined litigation and legal counseling with study and research without abandoning the transcendental values so necessary in life.

Dante Figueroa graduated with a law degree, with honors, from the University of Concepción in 1992. After joining the Chilean Bar Association (1993), he embarked on an intense practice as a lawyer and legal consultant in Chile, in the Municipalities of Coquimbo (1993), and in Macul, Santiago (1994-1999), as well as for various public entities, such as the Livestock and Cattle Development Institute in La Serena, (1993-1994) and the Sanitary Services Company SA, Coquimbo (1993-1995). These experiences undoubtedly prepared him for his post-graduate studies at the American University Washington College of Law, where he obtained a LL.M. in International Legal Studies with an emphasis on Environmental Law, cum laude (1997); and at the University of Chile Law School in Chile, where he also obtained a LL.M. in International Law, with distinction (1999).

With his academic specialization, he continued his career in Chile as a legal consultant at: the Forestry Institute (1999); the National Environmental Commission (1998-2000); and the Agency for International Cooperation (1999-2000). He also worked as a Member of Grasty Quintana Majlis & Cia, a prominent law firm in Santiago (2000-2002).

His professional experience continued in Washington, DC in 2003 where he worked as a: Law Fellow at the Center for International Environmental Law; Law Clerk at the Legal Aid Society of the District of Columbia (2003-2004); Contributing Editor and Attorney for the Environmental Law Institute (2004-2005); Legal Consultant to The George Muñoz Law Firm in Arlington, Virginia (2004-March 2006). From 2006 to the present day, he serves as the Senior Legal Analyst for the Law Library of the U.S. Congress. He has been able to accomplish his transcontinental professional activity given to his admittance to the New York Bar (2003), the D.C. Bar (2008), and the Supreme Court of the United States Bar (2013).

During his work in Washington, D.C. as Senior Legal Information Analyst at the Law Library of Congress, Dante Figueroa has developed an important bibliographical body of literature discussing laws, treaties, regulations, court decisions, and international legal principles involving several Latin American jurisdictions. While in Washington, D.C. Professor Figueroa has also served as Secretary General of the Inter-American Bar Association, where he promoted and defended the legal profession in the Southern Hemisphere.

As a consummate jurist, Professor Figueroa has pursued extensive academic activity parallel to the development of his professional activities. During his days as a student, he worked as an International Public Law Academic Assistant at the University of Concepcion Chile Law School (1991). In 1995, he was appointed Professor of International Public Law and Maritime Law at the Catholic University of the North Law School, La Serena, Chile. Then, in 1998, he taught Introduction to U.S. Law as an Assistant Professor at the University of Chile Law School. In 1999-2000, he taught Economic Law at the Christian Humanism University Law School, and in 2001-2002, he taught Environmental Law at the Republic University Law School. Since 2004, he has held a position as an Adjunct Professor of Law at the American University, Washington College of Law, located in Washington, D.C., where he has taught courses on Business Transactions in Latin America, Trade & Investment in Latin America, and U.S. Contract Law. Further, since 2010, he has regularly taught as an Adjunct Professor of Latin American Law at Georgetown University Law Center.

Dante Figueroa has written extensively on various topics of legal science, many discussing specific questions under private law, arbitration or environmental law. Some of his works can be considered as background of this work, in particular his work on Twenty-One Theses on the Legal Legacy of the French Revolution in Latin America, 39 Ga. J. Int'l & Comp. L. 29 (2010); his study on Proposals for a Re-Definition of the

Constitutional Basis for the Government Based on Natural Law in Latin America, published by Ars et Boni Aequi in Chile (2011); and his article on the "State of Nature" and the Philosophers of Law, in particular Edmund Burke," published in the Journal of Law of the Catholic University of the Holy Conception (2012).

With such training and experience, there is no one better than Professor Dante Figueroa to undertake the task of writing this book. Figueroa honors me with his request to present this work, which effortlessly synthesizes the evolution of the concept of natural law understood as "moral law accessible to all human beings through reason" (O'Scanniain), through the study of the perceptions concerning its fundamental definitions and components throughout the millennia prior to the emergence of modern Constitutional Law. With this purpose, Figueroa reminds us of the Greek notion of natural law as "intimately attached to the human person and inextricably united to the Eternal and Immutable Creator," and of the Roman notion of the law of nature which noted that "[b]ecause humans are part of nature, they are bound to its laws, which they cannot escape or alter". Finally, his book reflects on the Roman Catholic notion of natural law, linked to the "idea of a superior, eternal natural law," and codified by the Ten Commandments, "very much in harmony with Roman law, and in particular, with the Twelve Tables". The Roman notion of natural law, as Figueroa points out, is not only superior but is unchangeable, or as Thomas Aquinas said, "created by God it cannot change because God is unchangeable".

Based on this approach, Figueroa also reminds us of what he considers "one of Aquinas' greatest intellectual contributions," via his explanation about the legitimacy of positive (human) law vis-à-vis the natural law; sustaining that if positive law does not conform to the natural law, "it is not law at all and cannot bind in conscience". Since the law is "reason, not mere arbitrary will ...the natural law remains the measure of the positive law".

When referring to the Catholic doctrine of natural law according to the Spanish Scholastics, Figueroa points out that the Catholic doctrine contains three basic ideas that are essential for understanding the traditional concept of natural law: (a) "the notion of an eternal or divine law, that is, of a personal God as Lawgiver in the absolute sense;" (b) the idea of man as a blend of matter and soul and the transcendence of the soul; and (c) the idea of the Catholic Church as the supreme earthly interpreter in matters of faith and morals "above the will of the state, which arises from its mission as a vessel for salvation of souls".

From Chapter II onward, Figueroa studies what he considers the "monumental distortion" of "the true concept of natural law" that occurred, in his view, first with the Renaissance, and then with the French Revolution. He analyzes such "monumental distortion" of "Re-Foundational Attempts Against Traditional Natural Law" through the writings of the authors of the Enlightenment. From the era of Modern Rationalism-Humanism, he studies Grotius; Pufendorf; and Spinoza. From the Utilitarianism era he notes the work of Tomasius, Hume, Bentham, and Paine. And from the realm of Positivism, he analyzes the works of Kant. From all these authors new concepts arose, such as those of the state of nature, natural reason, natural theology, and natural ethics, which in his opinion ended up substituting "the notions of traditional natural law" for a new philosophy based on the notions of representative democracy, democratic government, popular sovereignty, separation between church and state, and the declaration of inalienability of individual rights, which eventually permeated Western constitutionalism.

In this process, Figueroa analyses the unparalleled influence of the writings of John Locke, the father of the "natural rights" doctrine that replaced the traditional natural law doctrine. Despite Locke's undeniable influence, Figueroa considers Locke a "master of confusion" based on Locke's attempts to justify his reasoning on men's "state of nature" as the "state of perfect freedom to order their [men's] actions and dispose of their possessions ... within the bounds of the law of nature," and further sustaining that men "by nature [are] all free, equal, and independent". Locke contributed to the principle of the radical separation between religion and civil government, which – combined with the French Revolution– became the ground of Western Constitutionalism.

I will not refer to the central aspects of this book; in particular, to the inroads of the "natural rights" theory into the Founding Documents of the United States, and to the search for the natural law notions that inspired the Founding Fathers; limiting myself to make a brief reference to the same efforts made towards the development of modern constitutionalism in Hispanic America.

At the beginning of the nineteenth century, the Founding Fathers of the new republics arising from the demise of the ancient Spanish colonies were, without doubt, inspired by the same principles that shaped North American constitutionalism, including those derived from the American Revolution itself. The Latin America Founding Fathers faced a completely different and difficult task of confronting the Catholic Church, which was completely compromised of the Spanish Absolute Monarchy. At the time of Independence, the Church openly condemned the efforts to establish new republics in Hispanic America, declaring all republicans its enemies. Such was the reason for the prohibition of even the classical Christian doctrine, such as what was considered Thomas Aquinas' "Jesuitical doctrine", in seminaries and universities throughout Latin America.

That is why after the first outbreaks of Independence occurred in Venezuela and Nueva Granada (1810), Pope Pius VII issued in 1816, under pressure by the Holy Alliance, the Encyclical *Etsi longissimo*, in which he asked for the complete destruction of the "fatal riots and insurrections that the enemy man sowed in those countries". He asked the clerics to show their congregations the "terrible and grave harms arising from rebellion and of the illustrious and singular virtues of Our Dear Jesus Christ Son, Fernando, Our Catholic King". Pope Pius VII pleaded the clerics to work hard in order to "strongly encourage the fidelity and obedience owed to our King".

Consequently, the Founding Fathers in Hispanic America not only had the enormous task of designing and building the constitutional framework of new Republics, based on the principles of Modern Constitutionalism derived from the North American and French revolutions, but also fought to refute the false religious arguments in favor of Absolute Monarchy and against the principles of representative democracy, democratic government, popular sovereignty, separation between church and state, and the declaration of inalienability of individual rights.

One of these exceptional men, Juan Germán Roscio, a lawyer with profound Catholic convictions, heavily contributed in the drafting of the 1811 Declaration of Independence of Venezuela and of the 1811 Federal Constitution of the Provinces of Venezuela, which was the first Modern Constitution in Latin America. I want to briefly refer, as a form of contribution to Figueroa's book, to Roscio's work, relying my comments on one of the few authors that has analyzed Roscio works: professor Luis Ugalde SJ, *El pensamiento teleológico-político de Juan Germán Roscio*, Caracas 2007; and on my own research for the edition of my book: *Constitutional Documents of the Independence of Venezuela 1811*, Caracas 2012, which contains the facsimile edition of the book: *Interesting Official Documents Relating to the United Provinces of Venezuela, London 1812)*, that Roscio helped to write and edit.

Roscio not only was one of the drafters of the basic documents of the independence of Venezuela, but had important functions within the new Venezuelan government. Roscio first served as a member "in representation of the people" of the *Junta Suprema* that overthrew the Spanish Colonial Governor in 1810, and subsequently served as the Minister of Foreign Affairs. In 1811, Roscio was elected member of the new Congress; for which he was persecuted from 1812 until 1815 as one of the "eight monsters responsible for all the evils in America", and suffered imprisonment in Ceuta, a Spanish enclave in the Northern coast of Africa. After his release, he managed to travel to Philadelphia, where in 1817 the Thomas H. Palmer printing house published his extraordinary book writen while in prison titled: *El Triunfo de la Libertad sobre el Despotismo, o la confesión, de un picador arrepentido de sus errores políticos, y dedicado a desagraviar en esta parte a la religión ofendida con el sistema de la tiranía*. In the book, Roscio identified himself as "a citizen of Venezuela in the America of the South". Although the book was never printed in Venezuela, by 1857 it had been reprinted three times in Philadelphia and three times in Mexico, where it even influenced the thinking of Benito Juárez. The work of Roscio is little known in the contemporary world, including in Venezuela.

In his remarkable book, Roscio explicitly assumed the Christian biblical and teleological justification of the republican independence as a necessary means to confront false religious and political ideas that surmised that republican independence was an attack against God, against his Holy religion, and as an act against the King of Spain, surely an act against God. The Christian theological and biblical justifications of the republic independence, on the contrary, were to be used to arise against Spanish despotism, discard it, and to found the system of independence.

In this regard, Roscio devoted his work to prove that the Catholic religion was being manipulated to be regarded as compatible with Tyranny. He assumed such task, based precisely on the principles of natural law, which demonstrates that a God supporting tyranny was not the God of the Bible, and that such was not the fate of Christians. Roscio considered that "nothing was more contrary to the books of religion, more chocking and advised against the precepts of the Gospels, and more repugnant to the natural and divine law" than the continuity of the enslaving and misery of the Americans. He based his arguments in a few basic ideas: (a) that certain evidences and axioms that are present in Nature are derived from God; (b) that all men are inviolable and sacred in their conditions of sons of God; (c) that men "are naturally free, so their liberty cannot be deprived except by just cause;" (d) that "freedom of men can only be diminished based on the consideration of a greater good that he himself intends upon entering society;" (e) that all power that is not derived from society "is tyrannical and illegitimate;" (f) that "all power is instituted for the benefit of the governed, not the governors;" (g) that "sovereignty has been and will always be a natural attribute, and inseparable from the people –Roscio considered this axiom– "a political and quasi-religious dogma".

Roscio concluded his liberal religious argument by presenting one of the central present ideas of classical scholasticism, that while the Bible says that all authority comes from God, and thus God is the first cause, that does not deny the sovereignty of the people as the second cause. From this reasoning, Roscio concludes that political power comes from God as an immediate cause, and from the people "as the immediate and visible source".

From his argumentation, Roscio derived his proposal, to which he devoted several chapters of his work, on the right of rebellion, in the sense that it dismantles the sacred fable of the absolute monarchy and demonstrated that inviolability is an attribute of every person. The People always have the right to rebel against the tyrants who oppress them and who deny them dignity. To that extent, he considered that it is "lawful to reject unjust aggression of a tyrant and the right to terminate overthrown him, if by no other luck security can be assured".

To justify such right, Roscio based his considerations on the Old Testament and on references to regicides contained in the Bible, as well as on Thomas Aquinas, who in his opinion "taught that it was lawful, and even mandatory, to destroy the tyrant and the governments who ruled tyrannically". Acquinas' text and doctrine, like I indicated before, were forbidden in Spanish America by the absolute monarchs. Therefore, Roscio said, "I speak of regicide by St. Thomas, by the natural and divine laws: regicide of a single name, being comprised in such doctrine, who because his tyrannical conduct can no longer be considered king".

The work by Dante Figueroa, that I have the pleasure and honor to present, as will surely be appreciated by the reader, analyzes the reasoning of the North American Founding Fathers regarding the idea of Natural Law. That is why I found as a way off paying homage to the author for the extraordinary study he offers us, to make reference to what the Founding Fathers of the Spanish American constitutionalism lived through decades after. These Founding Fathers had to face in their struggle for Independence not only an absolute monarchical power, which was pretended to be derivative of God, that ruled "by the grace of God," but also a Catholic Church whose agents defended tyranny and condemned any manifestation of freedom based on the notions of democratic representation, popular sovereignty, limited powers, human dignity, and the natural rights of man.

Hence the importance of the Roscio book aforementioned, which Guillermo E. Willwoll said "occupies a place entirely original and apart from all the writings of not only Venezuelans but American heroes, as its author was simultaneously a liberal and a sincere Catholic. We thus observe the originality of Roscio who purposefully tried to deal with the ideological relations between liberalism and Catholicism. He further strived to demonstrate the harmony between liberalism and the doctrine of the Catholic Church, and even the Bible" (William E. Willwoll, "Sesquicentennial of Juan Germán Roscius: Suárez-Rousseau-Roscius," in Journal of the Faculty of Law, Central University of Venezuela, Caracas 1974, p. 179).

New York, May 2014

PROLOGUE

Carlos José Errázuriz M.
Full Professor of Jurisprudence
Pontifical University of the Holy Cross (Rome)

Traditional Natural Law as the Source of Western Constitutional Law, Particularly in the United States is a work destined to educate law students on the topic. This clear and didactic endeavor involves great effort as it aims to achieve an authentic academic goal and constitutes a stimulus for the development of legal philosophical thinking. The author, Professor Dante Figueroa, is an Adjunct Professor at the Georgetown Law Center in Washington, D.C. His book constantly reveals the author's passion to capture and convey the truth. Precisely for this reason, the book transcends the circle of its immediate audience.

The basic thesis is perfectly synthesized in the title of the book. All the chapters attend to a common goal: to demonstrate that the traditional natural law and Western constitutional law are not, as it may be believed, two separate worlds; the first belonging to philosophers, theologians and historians, and the second to jurists. It shows that the tradition of natural law is relevant today for Western constitutional law, particularly in the United States - an approach that breaks with all preconceived models.

The key postulate of the book pivots around the doctrine of natural law. The book distinguishes between the authentic view of the doctrine, that the author qualifies as 'traditional'– whose origins are found in ancient Greece and Rome and has found its paradigmatic expression in Saint Thomas of Aquinas and the Spanish scholastics; and the deformations of that perspective, which the author situates particularly in the context of the Illumination and utilitarianism under the category of the "natural rights theories". Multiple elements differentiate both positions: namely, whether tradition is appreciated or rejected; whether transcendence ought to be harbored or expelled from the world of law; whether the divine character of natural law should be recognized, and whether natural law should be subordinated to positive law or otherwise; whether human society should be understood as something natural, or as the fruit of a social contract, based on a previous state of a social nature; what is the true sense of authority, and whether authority finds its foundation and limits in natural law, and thus rebellion against unjust authority is justified, or whether authority should be conceived as an expansion of popular sovereignty in its majoritarian expression; whether rights should be affirmed as something real and per se just, or rather as an abstract invocation of rights in the name of equality that serves to defend any interest.

The scheme just described does not pretend to be historically rigid, the author is well aware that in reality ideas mix. Thus it is very interesting, for example, to read the author's analysis of John Locke's thinking, in whom the distortion of the traditional perspective cohabits with acceptance of some of its aspects. On the other hand, the scheme evidences that it is not possible to simplify the whole spectrum of philosophical ideas about law by dividing them into iusnaturalists and positivists. To understand positivism, it is imperative to first understand the distorted iusnaturalism, which is its immediate precedent.

Figueroa speaks constantly about traditional natural law. This could create the impression that his prism is traditionalist; that is, anchored to a past that is considered irremovable by the reestablishment it seeks. But this view is equivocal; the author sees natural law as a reality that is current and valid. The author is not a nostalgic of the past but is convinced that there is a doctrinal patrimony that is transmitted and whose value derives from its adequacy to the truth about man and about God. At the same time, the author highlights those of the Catholic faith who have deepened these topics with greater success. Again, we must guard against the idea that we are before a cultural product of a confessional character. It is rather the synchrony with the truth −above all natural truth− that the Catholic faith has favored, precisely for its openness to the universality and depth of the message of Christ. The Catholic faith values everything in this patrimony that, thanks to the gifts of nature and grace, reaches all men and particularly other Christians.

The author habitually associates the distortions of the natural law doctrine with the natural rights theory. At the same time, the author is well aware that in the traditional view there is an affirmation of the true rights of the person. What he strongly rejects is a subjectivist and abstract perspective of rights that leads to the assertion of any rights. In this sense, I think it would have been useful to the author to take the conception of *ius into more* consideration; namely, the notion expressed by Saint Thomas of Aquinas in the formula *"ipsa res iusta"*. It is in this way that rights are objectified, considered as actual property attributed to persons, and also to the communities which demand respect and implementation from others.

I hope this book will contribute to a re-discovery of the fecundity and authentic modernity of a tradition which should shape constitutional law, all the other branches of government; and above all, the relationships be-tween persons and with society-in accordance with their dimension of jus-tice, rooted above all on natural law. Amongst the factors that unite me to the author, besides our dedication to the law and our common visn of life, is our shared Chilean origins: from them, I perceive with satisfaction his love towards the United States, and his interest in its history and its cur-rent state as a nation. I believe that this work will be fruitful primarily in the United States, but I also think that it will likely be useful in other con-texts.

Rome, November 19, 2013

INTRODUCTION

This work seeks to present to my students the essential concepts, elements, and reasoning indispensable for a true understanding of the connections between Western Constitutional law and Traditional Natural Law (*jus naturale*), in a way that is –hopefully– devoid of the many historical and remarkably entrenched prejudices that currently permeate the discipline of Constitutional Law in the West, particularly in the United States.

For the aforementioned purpose, this work will pointedly focus on the evolution of the perceptions concerning the fundamental definitions and components of Natural Law throughout the millennia before the emergence of modern Constitutional Law; as well as explain how this discipline must rid itself from the superfluous, twisted, or incomplete explanations of Natural Law that have polluted its core elements in the Western world, particularly since the Enlightenment.

The belief of Natural Law presupposes a religious creed; that is, the conviction that man is not simply a material being, but an amalgam of body and spirit that do not exclude one another. Indeed, the existence of God and the spirituality of the soul are accessible to human reason, despite and beyond the fallen nature of the human person. Equally, the religious *substratum* underlying the idea of Western constitutional law holds the conception that the spirit animates the body, and that both –body and spirit, spirit and body– were created by a Merciful and Omnipotent God who lay out rules governing both dimensions of man.

As all things human are *per se* complex and filled with unknowns, so is the relationship between the Traditional Natural Law Doctrine and its hybrid derivative, the Doctrine of Natural Rights. While the former is a uniform, complete, and coherent exposition of the discipline, the latter –which was popularized by the Enlightenment and had its apogee in the 18th century during the American Revolution– is a desultory potpourri incorporating veritable elements with unconvincing ones.

In consequence, this work argues that only a sound and decisive return to the genuine teachings of the originators of Western Natural Law, coupled with a healthy shaking off of its existing perturbing elements, will allow Western Constitutional Law to regain its majesty and thus earn a well-deserved respect from the Western masses, which will ultimately allow the democratic experiment to last.

CHAPTER I:

GENERAL OVERVIEW OF NATURAL LAW

The concept of natural law has received many definitions throughout the ages stemming from the philosophical background of its components. An accessible and workable definition is that natural law is the "moral law accessible to all human beings through reason".[1]

Since ancient times, Roman law "discovered" that certain things naturally belonged to all (for instance, the air, the ocean, certain lands, and animals) and therefore, had to be held in common. Other things, in turn, were susceptible to private, exclusive appropriation. This "natural" difference was thought to be discoverable by "'natural reason' and was deemed sufficient to dictate the structure of legal rights".[2] In practical terms, there are many institutions that are "natural" to man, namely, that are so interconnected and logical to humanity that they are necessarily present beyond geographical or temporal differences.

Despite its apparent remoteness, Roman law still pervades many of the fundamental legal institutions of common law. For example, as has been pointed out, the "basic features of the English and American law of capture"[3] come directly from Roman law.[4] Similarly, the notion of "possession" as the basal source of the right to acquire property or of personal work as a justification to keep what has been obtained by one's own toil comes from Roman law.[5] In this sense, the ultimate foundation of both

---

[1]   Diarmuid F. O'Scannlain, *The Natural Law in the American Tradition*, 79 Fordham L. Rev. 1513, 1521 (2011).

[2]   Richard A. Epstein, *The Modern Uses of Ancient Law*, South Carolina Law Review, Volume 48, Winter 1997, Number 2, at 245.

[3]   *Id.* at 246.

[4]   John Locke refers to the absurdity of denying a man his right to capture a wild animal while letting him starve, which goes against the natural principle of the right to self-preservation (*See* John Locke, The Second Treatise of Government (Dover Publications, Inc. Mineola, New York, 2002).

[5]   Epstein, *supra note* 2, at 247.

civil and common law springs from the same fountain of Roman law; what is considered as *ratio scripta*, that is, codified reason. Indeed, if the argument were made that the institutions of property and possession simply arise from positive (human) law, then such an argument would entail the irrationality that possession might not be a source of property in certain places or *époques*;[6] and that certain persons would have an exclusive right to possess things that nature offers to all, such as the oceans or the air, to the absolute exclusion of the rest of humanity.

Even the ancient philosophers argued for the legitimacy of property, believing that property increased "largely by wisdom, industry, and thrift and rightly belongs to its acquirer".[7] The same reasoning applies to the binding force of legally-agreed contractual obligations, *i.e.*, that the parties' free consent is a legitimate source for the enforcement of contractual rights. The natural law origins of the quasi-contract doctrine (called "unjust enrichment" under the American system) are also evident, in that nobody is entitled to freely benefit from the work of another.

For both civil and common law,[8] these rules find their ultimate source, historically and remotely, in Roman law and with logical immediacy in human reason, all of which are elements more properly understood as "natural law".

1. Traditional Natural Law: A Discipline Uncovered, Expounded, and Sustained Throughout the Ages by Catholic Writers

It has been rightly stated that "[t]he doctrine of natural law is as old as philosophy".[9] The primeval question that natural law seeks to respond is whether "the moral basis of human laws [as well as] the problem of why laws are binding".[10]

---

[6] The U.S. Supreme Court has expressly recognized this "natural right" to possession of wild animals by holding that "it was self-evident (that is, a matter of natural reason) that wild animals can only be owned by the state when it, like any private party, first reduces them to possession." (Epstein, *supra note* 3, at 252, referring to Douglas v. Seacoast Prods., Inc., 431 U.S. 265, 284 (1977).

[7] Jude P. Dougherty, Property as a Condition of Liberty, *in* Fellowship of Catholic Scholars Quarterly (Number 2, Summer 2011), at 10 (citing Cicero).

[8] Epstein, supra *note* 2, at 249 ("the origins of this conception lie in Roman law.").

[9] Heinrich A. Rommen, The Natural Law. A Study in Legal and Social History and Philosophy (Arno Press, New York, 1979), Part I, The History of the Idea of Natural Law, at 3.

[10] *Id.* at 4.

In the early third century, Tertullian was the first Catholic author to use the term "natural law".[11] By the fourth century, St. Augustine of Hippo had already taught that, "the eternal law is the divine order or will of God, which requires the preservation of natural order, and forbids the breach of it".[12] In this manner, St. Augustine identified several essential elements of natural law: (i) that there is an eternal and immutable law given by God to humankind; (ii) that this divine law provides a natural order for the functioning of the universe and of mankind; and (iii) that this natural order may not be violated by man without offending the eternal law, that is, God Himself.

The "moral" connotation given to natural law via the reference to "natural moral law" involves an allusion to

the light of reason inherent in us by nature, through which we perceive what we ought to do and avoid; or also the knowledge, communicated to us by the Creator through nature, that we must strictly observe in our conduct the order which corresponds to our nature.[13]

While the natural order "is an order of absolute necessity for unfree creatures ... it is also an order of oughtness, a moral order, for rational and free beings".[14] That is to say, while brute animals lack free will and cannot "opt out" of the natural order; man –a creature with free will– has the possibility of "opting out" of the natural order. Thus man's law is a moral law of freedom.

Accordingly, this Chapter reviews the true concept of natural law as it was known to the Western intellect until its monumental distortion; first, at the hands of the Renaissance and then at those of the French Revolution.[15] Starting in the seventeenth century, the notions of traditional natural law were substituted by the "philosophy, light, liberality, and the rights

---

[11]   Libero Gerosa, I *Introduzione al Diritto Canonico* 41 (Lib. Editrice Vaticana, 2012).

[12]   Rommen, *supra note* 9, at 180.

[13]   *Id.* at 181-2.

[14]   *Id.* at 180.

[15]   Commission Théologique Internationale, *À la recherche d'une éthique universelle: Nouveau regard sur la loi naturelle* (Fr. Serge-Thomas Bonino, ed., 2009), at 10 ("Il est vrai que l'expression de « loi naturelle est source de nombreux malentendus dans le contexte actuel » ["It is true that the term 'natural law' is the source of many misunderstandings in the current context."]).

of men,"[16] ideology forcibly imposed after 1789. Though "full of false rhetoric,"[17] this liberal philosophy captivated the lower echelons of the Western intellect. It is only in this context that the birth of Western constitutionalism may be understood as the progeny of the cataclysmic consequences unleashed by the French Revolution. In effect, among the key ideas bred by the Revolution, which have permeated Western constitutionalism to this day, are: the notions of representative democracy, democratic government, popular sovereignty, separation between church and state,[18] and the declaration of inalienability of individual rights.[19] These concepts are reviewed later in this work.

2. *On the Origins of the Concept of Natural Law*

A. *Ancient Greek Thinkers*

The idea of a "natural law" pre-existent to positive law was present in the Ancient Greek culture.[20] In fact, the ancient Greeks were the first to posit the "philosophical conception of the natural law,"[21] based on an objective, or reasonable, proposition of justice-just is what accords to reason, and unjust is what is contrary to right reason.[22] In general terms, the Greek proposed two conceptions of the natural law: the Stoic and the Sophistic. Heraclitus of Ephesus first advanced the Stoic doctrine by recognizing the existence of a god as the "supreme lawgiver,"[23] that is, the *logos*. This divine lawgiver was thought as an unchangeable and eternal mind provid-

---

[16]   Edmund Burke, *Reflections on the Revolution in France*, (The Temple Press Letch worth, London, 1910 edition), at 113.

[17]   Edmund Burke, *Thoughts on French Affairs (December 1791)*, in Henry Rogers, *The Works of the Right Hon.* Edmund Burke, with a Biographical and Critical Introduction (London, 1848), at 580.

[18]   Friedrich Gentz, *The Origin and Principles of the American Revolution*, Compared with the Origin and Principles of the French Revolution (Peter Koslowski, Ed., Indianapolis, 2010), at VIII.

[19]   *Id.* at XVI.

[20]   Commission Théologique Internationale, *supra note* 16, at 18 (referring to the character Antigone −Aedipo's daughter− who, claiming from the King Creon the "natural right" to burial of her brother, alludes to "unwritten and immutable laws.").

[21]   Rommen, *supra note* 9, at 5.

[22]   Javier Hervada, *Cos'è il diritto? La moderna risposta del realismo giuridico* (Subsidia Canonica, ed. Roma, 2013), at 56.

[23]   Rommen, *supra note* 9, at 5.

ing a "universal reason"[24] to all things. Under the Stoic conception, human virtue and wisdom exist when the precepts of the "general law of the universe"[25] are followed, both individually and collectively. Furthermore, human laws are "but attempts to realize this divine law,"[26] from which they "draw their force,"[27] and which ought not to be resisted. In this way, Stoicism recognized a clearly objective ethical *substratum* to positive law.[28]

Pope Benedict XVI lucidly explained the importance of Stoicism for the formation of traditional natural law:

> In the first half of that century, the social natural law developed by the Stoic philosophers came into contact with leading teachers of Roman Law. Through this encounter, the juridical culture of the West was born, which was and is of key significance for the juridical culture of mankind.[29]

In contrast, the theory advanced by the Sophists propounded a notion of natural law pivoting around the idea of the State as "a social unit which rests upon a free contract [and which is] arbitrary and artificial [and is] determined by utility [and] not metaphysically necessary".[30] In the Sophists' positivistic view, laws "were artificial constructs and served the interests of the powerful".[31] Laws certainly ascribed to a notion of "natural rights," an affirmation that long preceded the disquisitions of the *philosophes* of the Enlightenment. In effect, in the Sophists' view, laws "possessed no inherent value, for only what is right by nature can have such value".[32] In general, the Sophistics' philosophical notions of natural rights were centered around the following ideas: (a) that "existing laws serve

---

[24]   *Id.* at 6.

[25]   *Id.*

[26]   *Id.*

[27]   *Id.*

[28]   Commission Théologique Internationale, *supra note* 16, at 21 ("Dans le stoïcisme, la loi naturelle devient le concept clef d'une éthique universaliste".–"According to Stoicism, the natural law becomes the core concept of an universalist ethics").

[29]   Comments taken from the Speech of the His Holiness Pope Benedict XVI to the Federal Parliament in the Reichstag Building, on September 22, 2011 (hereinafter the "Reichstag Speech"), *available at*: http://www.ewtn.com/papalvisitgermany/archive/visit Parliament0922.asp.

[30]   Rommen, *supra note* 9, at 5.

[31]   *Id.* at 8.

[32]   *Id.*

class interests and are artificial constructions";[33] (b) that there existed "rights of man as well as the idea of mankind … or world community",[34] in tandem with the idea of the "natural-law freedom and equality of all";[35] and (c) that the State is "nonessential [and] it owes its origin, to a human decision … to a free contract".[36] According to the Sophists, the State was an artificial being. The Sophistical way was more simplistic and invariably tended to slogans that overlooked the great philosophical and moral dilemmas ever present in the discussion on the validity of law. The metaphysical approach, instead, required a higher degree of sophistication.[37] Centuries later, John Locke would call the institution prior to the State the "state of nature".

In the seventeenth and early eighteenth centuries, John Locke resurrected the individualistic prism first advanced by the Sophists when he proclaimed that the "function of the state of nature and of the idea of natural law is to establish as inalienable the rights of the individual".[38] Locke was an architect of right, not of duty. He focused his explanations on the rights, aspirations, and selfish passions and perspectives of the individual. He sowed the seeds of modern Epicureanism[39] when he taught that, "[i]n private domestic affairs, in the management of estates, [and] in the conservation of bodily health, every man may consider what suits his own convenience, and follow what course he likes best".[40] The man without boundaries, responsibilities, or limitations was thus born.

In this individual-centric society, the "rights of individuals afford an ultimate criterion for judging all acts of the government and all laws of the state".[41] In that sense, the revival of Sophism in eighteenth century Europe was simply unsurprising. What was utterly astounding was the dialectic of

---

[33]   *Id.* at 9.

[34]   *Id.*

[35]   *Id.*

[36]   *Id.* at 9-10.

[37]   *Id.* at 7.

[38]   *Id.* at 88.

[39]   Edmund Burke, *Speech on the Second Reading of a Bill for the Relief of Protestant Dissenters* (1773), *in* Rogers, *supra note* 16, at 472 (referring to the Epicureans as "atheists [and] free-thinkers"). *Id.* at 473 (stating that "these atheists take advantage of the liberty of their foes to introduce irreligion.").

[40]   John Locke, *A Letter Concerning Toleration* (Dover Publications, Inc. Mineola, New York, 2002), at 127.

[41]   Rommen, *supra note*, at 89.

contradiction propounded by the enlightened *philosophes* between natural law and positive law,[42] and the zeal with which these ideas were received in the hearts of the enlightened philosophers.

Now, going back to Ancient Greece, Socrates was somehow caught in the middle of the Stoic and Sophistic perspectives. On the one hand, he affirmed the existence of a superior natural law, but at the same time he held a positivistic position in that all "laws of Athens [were] 'right' [meaning, "just'] without qualification".[43] Socrates also perceived the Sophists' "extreme rationalism,"[44] as dangerous and tending to the dissolution of morality, and as propounding a "mere rationalization of political interests".[45] Socrates, instead, taught universalities, that is, the existence of concepts and notions that are knowable to man based on reason: "goodness, beauty, and justice".[46]

The Epicureans arose as the intellectual heirs of the Sophists. However, contrary to the optimism of the Sophists, the Epicureans held a pessimistic view of the "artificial" State propounded by the Sophists. As a result, the Epicureans proposed that mere "utility" was the ultimate driving force and *raison d'être* of the State.[47] The Epicureans denied "that anything can be objectively and naturally right".[48] As a result, "utility and pleasure [are] the sole principles of ethics and law [and] justice thus consists entirely in positive laws".[49] We will see later that the ideologies of "Rousseau, Hobbes, Pufendorf, Thomasius, and [of] the adherents of historical schools of law"[50] are at their core nothing but a rehash of ancient Epicurenism.

Ethical considerations about the law dominated the thinking of Plato and Aristotle. According to them, positive laws are "generally good and constitute the implementation, more or less successfully, of a natural law in accordance to the nature of things".[51] In fact, their aim was to "establish

---

[42]   *Id.* at 250 ("[t]he positive law was the direct opposite of the law of nature").

[43]   *Id.* at 7.

[44]   *Id.* at 12.

[45]   *Id.* at 20.

[46]   *Id.*

[47]   *Id.*

[48]   *Id.*

[49]   *Id.*

[50]   *Id.* at 11.

[51]   Commission Théologique Internationale, *supra note* 15, at 20.

the ethical basis of the laws".[52] At the core of their doctrines was the distinction between "what is naturally just and what is legally just".[53] In other words, they rightly admitted that what is simply legal is not always teleologically just. The legitimacy of the law derives from its participation in the notion of eternal justice. Therefore, the "ideal concept becomes a norm,"[54] and positive laws "may claim legal force only [when they] partake of the idea of law".[55] The Platonic understanding of human nature views man "with impaired powers of contemplation,"[56] in contrast to the "optimism of the Sophists,"[57] for whom the "state, is not something eternal, nor is its law. It is mankind that is eternal".[58]

The idea of a higher, eternal source of the legitimacy of human law pervades Aristotle's and Socrates' legal thinking.[59] As a result, positive law is nothing but the "attempt to realize the natural law".[60] For Aristotle, the natural function of the judge is "filling up gaps in the law as an attempt to apply the natural law".[61] Consequently, these lacunae are "the gateways through which the natural law continually comes into play ... in accordance with the norm which the true lawgiver would himself apply if he were present".[62]

For the Skeptics, in turn, neither senses nor reason "guarantee the truth and the certitude of knowledge".[63] All laws are simply arbitrary since they are based neither on the senses nor in reason. Ultimately, in their view, since humans "cannot perceive the essence or nature of things and of man ... natural law is impossible".[64]

---

[52] Rommen, *supra note* 9, at 13.

[53] *Id.* at 15.

[54] *Id.* at 14.

[55] *Id.* at 15.

[56] *Id.*

[57] *Id.*

[58] *Id.* (finding that "natural law has its source in the essence of the just, in nature. That which is naturally right is therefore unalterable").

[59] *Id.* at 17.

[60] *Id.* at 18.

[61] *Id.*

[62] *Id.*

[63] *Id.* at 20.

[64] *Id.*

In synthesis, Ancient Greece planted the seeds for the notion of natural law as intimately attached to the human person and inextricably united to the Eternal and Immutable Creator. Catholic thinking later refined these ideas rescuing what was good and reasonable in them.[65]

Eventually, and "[u]nder the influence of Stoic philosophy the doctrine of the natural law passed into Roman law".[66] However, the ancient Greeks did not know the divine nature of human dignity and the ultimate transcendence of the human soul; neither did they know of the Catholic Church as a vessel for "the primordial personal goal of man [that is] his eternal happiness or the salvation of his soul".[67] Consequently, as we will review later, the ancient Greeks "failed to arrive at the distinction between natural law and natural moral law".[68]

B. *Pagan Roman Thinkers*

It has been often said that Stoicism proposed a natural law doctrine that "prepared the way for the Christian natural law".[69] Amongst Roman orators and jurists, Cicero occupies a central role as the great exponent of stoicism in the second century B.C..[70] In fact, many "passages of Roman law which touch the natural law have their source mostly in Stoic philosophical literature".[71] Several principles based on Stoic moral philosophy resonate to our modern ears: (a) the "unity of knowledge and conduct forms the ideal of the sage;"[72] (b) "[vi]rtue is right reason. Nature and reason are one. Right reason and the universal law of nature ... are also one;"[73] (c) as a consequence of its provenance, law "rests not upon the arbitrary will of a ruler or upon the decree of a multitude, but upon na-

---

[65] *Id.* at 26.

[66] *Id.*

[67] *Id.* at 238.

[68] *Id.* at 33.

[69] *Id.* at 21.

[70] Cicéron, *De legibus*, I, VI, 18 ("pour Cicéron la loi est "la raison suprême insérée dans la nature qui nous commande ce qu'il faut faire et nous interdit le contraire"– for Cicero, the law is 'the supreme reason inserted in nature that commands us what we must do, and prohibits us the opposite"), *cited* in Commission Théologique Internationale, *supra note* 16, at 21.

[71] Rommen, *supra note* 9, at 21.

[72] *Id.* at 22.

[73] *Id.*

ture;[74] and undoubtedly the most important Stoic ethical principle, (d) "[o]bedience to the eternal world law in a life lived according to reason".[75]

Cicero made some well-known references to the "law of nature" when he recognized that,

> Part of God's divine intelligence and the highest expression of reason, law regulates the universe and nature, as well as human societies and individual behavior. Because humans are part of nature, they are bound to its laws, which they cannot escape or alter. A well-regulated and lawful state is one that models its legal system after the laws of nature.[76]

Cicero also explained that "[true] law is right reason in agreement with nature; it is of universal application, unchanging and everlasting".[77] Further, Cicero explicitly excluded the majoritarian rule as the source of legitimacy of positive law:

> If the principles of Justice were founded on the decrees of peoples, the edicts of princes, or the decisions of judges, then Justice would sanction robbery and adultery and forgery of wills, *in case these acts were approved by the votes or decrees of the populace.*[78]

Thus, Roman thinkers developed even further the debate about the validity of positive law in the light of traditional natural law.

C. *Catholic Roman Thinkers*

The search for an early reference to natural law in the Christianized Roman legal thinking after the Decree of Constantine, results in numerous references to the *Corpus Iuris Civilis* as proof of the origin of the concept of natural law in the civil law tradition. The following are several of those well-noted references:

---

[74] *Id.* at 22-23.

[75] *Id.*

[76] John Poulakos, et al., *Classical Rhetorical Theory* (1999), Chapter 6 "Rhetoric in Rome," at 159.

[77] The Republic, III, XXII, trans. by C. W. Keyes, in The Loeb Classical Library), *cited* in Heinrich A. Rommen, *The Natural Law* ..., *supra note* 9, at 24, FN 12.

[78] Rommen, *supra note* 9, at 23 (emphasis added).

for just as freedom is part of natural law and slavery was introduced by the law of nations (*ius gentium*) so the question of whether there is a debt or not a debt is ... to be interpreted naturally".[79]

[B]y the law of nature it is fair that no one can be made richer by the loss and injury to another.[80]

The notion that this natural law is just runs parallel to the idea of a superior, eternal natural law. Interestingly, the Aristotelical/Socratical idea that judges fill in legislation gaps by recurring to the eternal law, and particularly the "Stoic idea of an eternal law of the order of the universe,"[81] made its way into Roman law through the idea of *aequitas* –the eternal law of justice that provides solutions to vacuums in the positive law by way of explanation of the magistrates. Roman jurists saw *aequitas* as the "echo of the *lex naturae*– natural law".[82] *Aequitas*, in consequence, became the "legal conscience"[83] of the Christianized Roman law.

It was thus left to the Roman jurists to define the "material contents of the law of nature".[84] The following are some examples of areas of positive Roman law that were gradually filled in by Roman magistrates appealing to the notion of *aequitas*:

kinship (marriage-family), good faith, adjustment or weighing of interests (*suum cuique*), the real meaning of the actual will of the legal subject as opposed to the formalism of the law governing expression of will. To these may be added the original freedom and equality of all men, and the right of self-defense (*vim vi repellere*).[85]

The Roman jurist Pomponius, quoted in the *Institutes* of Justinian, also recognized that natural law is that which nature instills in all animals, and is not peculiar to humankind but exists in all animals. From nature –Pomponius stresses– derives that association between man and woman that we call marriage,[86] and the consequent procreation and raising of children.

---

[79]   Alan Watson, *The Law of Reason*, *in* The Making of the Civil Law, Harvard University Press (1981), at 83-98.

[80]   Watson, *supra note* 79, at 83-98.

[81]   Rommen, *supra note* 9, at 27.

[82]   *Id.*

[83]   *Id* at 28.

[84]   *Id.*

[85]   *Id.*

[86]   *Id.* at 238 ("[t]he family and its basis, marriage, are prior to the state").

Therefore, Pomponious concludes, natural law is the law that is common to all human beings. And, there is another law that pertains to certain peoples only, what the Romans termed "Roman Civil Law" or the Law of the Quirites.[87] The same "naturalness" is found in parental rights,[88] the inevitability of the state as a political unity,[89] and the love of country through the criminalization of treason.[90] The famous Roman jurist Ulpian, who defined natural law as "that which nature teaches to all animals,"[91] went a step further and added several other principles common to all peoples and nations, including, the principles of obedience to parents and country; as well as, the rejection of violence and wrong, e.g. "it is wrong for man to ambush man". The recognition of this natural character was extended to present day international law.[92]

In sum, the Stoic ideas about the natural character of "the family, the local community [and] the nation [as] enduring institutions,"[93] were widely recognized by the most important Roman legal minds and passed to scholasticism in the Middle Ages. In effect, the Spanish Scholastics later bundled all these intellectual constructions as a discipline called "natural law", and filled them in, creating new meaning. Namely, the Scholastics explained that the Ten Commandments were "codified natural law," very much in harmony with Roman law, and in particular, with the Twelve Tables, the Roman codification of the fifth century.

Notwithstanding the greatness of the Christianized Roman legal references to natural law, the systematic and coherent identification of the distinction between law and morality"[94] came to be explained only by the Spanish Scholastics.[95]

---

[87]   Watson, *supra note* 79, at 83-98.

[88]   Rommen, *supra note* 10, at 239 ("parents, especially the father, have natural rights which the positive law does not confer upon them, but which, as already existent, it protects and guarantees").

[89]   *Id.* at 240. ("[I]ndividuals are not free to unite or not to unite to form a state [but] the natural moral law imposes such union").

[90]   *Id.* ("the betrayal of one's nationality is a crime. This is true even if no penal code of a state").

[91]   *Id.* at 29 (quod natura omnia animalia docuit).

[92]   *Id.* at 242 ("[T]he positive international law also has its foundation in the natural law").

[93]   *Id.* at 244.

[94]   *Id.* at 29.

[95]   *Id.* at 30.

D. *Canon Law*

The first compilation of Canon law effectuated by the Gratian *Decretum* of 1148 famously referred to *"ius naturae quod in Evangelio et lege* [the natural law is found in the Gospels and the Law-Decalogue]".[96] Hence, the Decalogue contains the essence of the natural moral law, which prohibits "theft, lying, adultery, and perjury" because these conducts "are intrinsically evil".[97]

The Gratian *Decretum* further distinguished between *ius naturale* –natural law– and customs (customary law). While *ius naturale* was "contained in the Law (*i.e.*, the Decalogue) and the Gospels, [and] is of divine origin [...] resides in human nature [and] has force independently of human statute".[98] Customary law, in turn, "change(s) according to time, place, and people".[99] Changeability, not intrinsic moral character, is then the central difference between natural law and customary law. The later demonization of customary law finds its roots in the Enlightenment, which gave birth to the French Revolution,[100] not in traditional natural law.

3. *Thomas Aquinas (1225-1274)*

Undoubtedly, traditional natural law is a discipline developed, expounded, matured, and taught by Catholic thinkers. Thomas Aquinas, who is first and foremost a Saint of the Catholic Church, was the prime thinker to coherently propose and systematize the "doctrine of the immutability of the natural law"[101] as the *Lex Aeterna Dei* [Eternal Law of God]. In fact, he proposed "the doctrine of the priority of the intellect over the will in God as well as in man [as] a prerequisite of the possibility of a natural moral law".[102] In his normative pyramid, the basis of natural moral law resides in the priority of existence over knowledge and of knowledge over will.[103]

---

[96] *Id.* 65.

[97] *Id.*

[98] *Id.* at 38.

[99] *Id.* at 39.

[100] Dante Figueroa, Twenty-One Theses on the Legal Legacy of the French Revolution in Latin America, 39 Ga. J. Int'l & Comp. L. 29 (2010), at 60.

[101] Rommen, *supra note* 9, at 168.

[102] *Id.* at 177.

[103] *Id.* at 198.

Indeed, for Thomas Aquinas "law" is a *rationis ordinatio*, that is, rational ordering[104] emanating from legitimate authority, aimed at the common good, and promulgated.[105] Therefore, the role of judges is "not to correct legislatures for being defective philosophers or defective anthropologists, but rather for passing positive laws that are fatally defective as laws".[106] In this view that still resonates contemporaneously, these defects might be procedural —for instance, lack of proper authority or promulgation; or substantive— such as, forcing citizens to do something morally or physically impossible or positing contradictory or illogical obligations.

For Aquinas, positive (or human) law is a "specification or particularrized instantiation of the natural law;"[107] and consequently, an emanation of natural law.[108] The logical consequence is that there exist certain rights inherent to the human person at both the individual and collective levels that "pre-date" positive law. In other words, there are rights that the State, the government, or society has —through positive law embodied in either the Constitution or legislation— not "granted" or "given" to the human person. On the contrary, these rights have only been recognized by those collectivities whose only *reason d'être* is to guarantee the sound enjoyment of such rights.

For Aquinas, a contradiction between belief and reason as the foundation of positive law is a *non sequitur*. He explicitly states that "[l]aw is "first and foremost an act of reason,"[109] and "directs the actions of free man to the common good".[110] The fact that law must follow reason neces-

---

[104]   *Id.* at 172 ("[t]he world is order. The order of creatures according to the differentiation of their natures and their gradations proceeds from God's wisdom. Chance is not the origin of things, nor is the world a chaos").

[105]   Michael Baur, *Beyond Standard Legal Positivism and "Aggressive" Natural Law: Some Thoughts on Judge O'scannlain's "Third Way,"* 79 Fordham L. Rev. 1529, 1541 (2011) (this paper was written in response to Judge O'Scannlain, Diarmuid, supra *note* 1).

[106]   *Id.* at 1536.

[107]   *Id.* at 1538.

[108]   St. Thomas of Aquinnas, Cf. *Quaestiones disputatae de veritate*, q. 12, a. 3, ad 11 ("Iustitia vero per quam gubernatur societas humana in ordine ad bonum civile, sufficienter potest haberi per principia iuris naturalis homini indita" ["The justice by which human society is governed in order for the good of the city, can be obtained through the principles of natural law implanted in man"]).

[109]   Rommen, *supra note* 9, at 198.

[110]   *Id.* at 194.

sarily means that law must "be in conformity with truth".[111] In other words, a law may not retain its character of law if it codifies falsities. It logically follows that when positive law conforms to natural law, it is fitting for man to unequivocally abide by the law.[112]

Now, let us systematize further Aquinas' main ideas on natural law: [113]

A. *Understanding and Free Will Distinguish Man From Other Animals*

This obvious reality is for Aquinas a consequence of man having been created in "the image and likeness of God".[114] As God is supreme understanding and will –even in the view of the ancient Greek philosophers– man, his creation, is gifted with these same twin ontological features.

B. *The Created World Reflects the Will of the Creator*

For Aquinas, the "essential nature of the created world"[115] is but a reflection of the intent of its Creator. That is to say, the universe functions according to rules willed by God, and that ordering of things constitutes the normal way of how they should function, *i.e.*, their natural order. Hence, being and oughtness coincide in natural law precisely according to God's will.

There are several dimensions of this natural law created and willed by God: (a) the laws of natural sciences; (b) the laws of evolution and growth in living creatures (animals and plants);[116] and (c) the laws of "theoretical and practical reason"[117] that govern man.

Therefore, man obeys natural law because he ought to do it according to the natural state and being of things, and not just out of "blind compulsion and necessity".[118]

---

[111]   *Id.* at 195.

[112]   *Id.* at 192 ("[L]aw is a rule and measure of acts, whereby man is induced to act or is restrained from acting.").

[113]   *Id.* at 218 (interestingly, Aquinas showed a genuine interest in "extensive studies in comparative law.").

[114]   *Id.* at 45.

[115]   *Id.*

[116]   *Id.* at 46.

[117]   *Id.* at 45.

[118]   *Id.* at 46.

C. *Reason as the Compass to Determine the Morality of an Action*

According to Aquinas, "reason is the first and proximate rule for judging the moral quality of an action".[119] The reasonable will is directed to goodness and abides by the natural order of things. Then, the natural law is good and reasonable. If the law is good, as already stated, law is also true since nothing that is false can be good.

However, and this is a crucial difference between Aquinas and the enlightened philosophers, in Aquinas' thinking human reason is "never the [ultimate] criterion of truth".[120] Despite its lofty place in the pyramid of the human dimension, neither reason or intellect is aided by the senses in order for man to gain understanding.[121] Man does not gain knowledge and understanding by either reason or the senses alone.[122] A cooperative interaction between reason and senses reflect the true dimension of human nature and lead man to his ultimate goals.

D. *To Pursue Good and Avoid Evil is the*
Summary of the Natural Moral Law

The supreme commandment of the natural moral law is that "[g]ood is to be done, evil is to be avoided".[123] Actions, when they correspond to the essential nature of things, "are in themselves good, moral, just"[124] because they accord to natural law, and therefore ought to be permitted by human (positive) law. On the contrary, if actions do not correspond to the essential nature of things, they do not accord to natural law and ought to be prohibited by human law.

---

[119] *Id.* at 47.

[120] *Id.* at 87.

[121] *Id.* at 164 ("[T]he intellect alone does not understand ... nor do the senses alone perceive").

[122] *Id.* at 165 ("[A] thing is not known through the senses, but through the intellect with the aid of the senses").

[123] *Id.* at 51.

[124] *Id.* at 50.

E. *Natural Law is Immutable*

As natural law is created by God it cannot change because God is unchangeable.[125] This reality is easily perceivable, for instance, in the formulation of the first three commandments of the Decalogue. In fact, they required "special promulgation [since] they are not so evident as the laws found in the second table (last seven commandments)".[126] In effect, the last seven commandments "are derived from the mutual relations among men and from the essence and goal of human nature,"[127] namely: (a) the protection of family and parental authority (fourth commandment); (b) the protection of human life (fifth commandment); (c) preservation of marital life of husband and wife (sixth commandment); (d) the right of property (seventh commandment); and (e) honor (eighth commandment). The last two commandments prohibit "inordinate, illicit longing for those goods which are especially exposed to covetousness".[128]

Obviously, and regrettably due to man's fallen state, "the natural law can be blotted out from the human heart, either by evil persuasions ... or by vicious customs and corrupt habits".[129] In that regard, self-education and un-checked personal inclination to goodness are not sufficient guarantees to preserve social order-positive law and public institutions are necessary to govern man in his fallen state. Accordingly, the role of positive law is to maintain order and to correct human behavior; thus "render[ing] the citizen virtuous".[130]

On the other hand, to admit that the natural law −which is eternal− might be changed, is to admit that natural law is imperfect, or that it is able of achieving perfection. That would imply a denial of natural law's absolute goodness, and thus would to render it imperfect. In sum, since nothing that is absolutely true is perfectible, natural law may only be deemed to be perfect in its regulations, as it is willed by God, who is absolute perfection Himself.

---

[125] *Id.*

[126] *Id.* at 52.

[127] *Id.*

[128] *Id.*

[129] Summa theologica, Ia Hae, q.94. a.6. cr. ibid., q.77. a.a: q.94. a.5; *cited* in Rommen, *supra note* 10, FN 19, at 53.

[130] Rommen, *supra note* 9, at 54.

F. *To Be Legitimate, Human Law Must Conform to Natural Law*

Perhaps one of Aquinas' greatest intellectual contributions was his explanation about the legitimacy of positive (human) law vis-à-vis natural law. He famously sustained that if positive law does not conform to natural law, "it is not law at all and cannot bind in conscience".[131] As the law is "reason, not mere arbitrary will ... the natural law remains the measure of the positive law".[132] Any law forcing an individual to do something that is prohibited by natural law, or prohibiting something that natural law permits, is an expression of tyranny, and is not binding at all because it is not a law. The immoral law is, therefore, "absolutely null and void".[133]

4. *The Beginning of the Distortions of Traditional Natural Law*

Aquinas' ink was still wet when writings distorting the right understanding of traditional natural law were in the works. One of the first deformations came from Duns Scotus (1266 - 1308), who proposed that, "morality depends on the will of God".[134] This simple, yet hurtful, statement wiped out at once the non-changeability of the natural law. To wit, to make morality dependent on will (even if it be God's will) leaves the door open to the possibility of an acceptance or rejection of the moral law. To state that God may will what is not moral (corrupt) is nothing but heresy in the old theological dictionary. It follows that if God may will what is corrupt; man, created in God's image and likeness, may also will what is corrupt without injuring the notion of justice and natural law. As we will see later, this relativization of the natural moral law began with apparently innocuous reasoning, such as Scotus,' and ended up corrupting the whole discipline of natural law in its authentic version.

But, it was William of Occam (1287-1347) who further damaged the traditional notion of natural law. He argued that besides the act of creation of man by God, there is "no unchangeable moral order grounded in the nature of things".[135] His assertion denied that actions are true and good *in themselves*. Instead, Occam advanced the tenuous argument that actions

---

[131] *Id.* at 55.

[132] *Id.* at 56.

[133] *Id.* at 66.

[134] *Id.* at 58.

[135] *Id.*

are good "because God so wills".[136] Sin is, therefore, no longer something that is *intrinsically* evil, but something that is only morally reproachable because it is "an external offense against the will of God".[137] There is here a total separation between "being, truth, and goodness".[138] In effect, since there is no unity between goodness and truth, God's will can change at any time and thus, the morality of actions depends on whether it adjusts to God's (eternally changing) will at a given time. As a result, "[l]aw is will, pure will without any foundation in reality".[139] In a sense, Occam identified the mere absolute will of the sovereign with the law and thus denied the existence of traditional natural law.[140] In this sense, Occam can be said to be the precursor of positivism since he dissolved the idea of natural law.[141] In overt opposition to Occam, the Spanish Scholastics proposed that, "God [only] wills that which accords with nature".[142]

5. *Spanish Scholasticism (from beginning of Sixthteenth Century)*

As already stated, the Roman ideas on natural law were processed with astonishing mastery by Catholic thinkers beginning with the Scholastic tradition initiated by St. Thomas of Aquinas in the thirteenth century and followed with the Spaniards Francisco Suárez and Francisco de Vitoria in the fifthteenth and sixthteenth centuries. Under the Spaniards, Classical (or Traditional) Natural Law obtained a central role in the civil law tradition. They developed a highly sophisticated theory of natural law that provided a crucial doctrinal stronghold against the "imperialist ideology of certain Christian European rulers and to defend the rights of the non-Christian peoples of the Americas".[143]

Pope Benedict XVI has clarified the intimate connection between traditional natural law and the Christian Scriptures:

---

[136] *Id.* at 59.

[137] *Id.*

[138] *Id.*

[139] *Id.*

[140] *Id.* at 60.

[141] *Id.* at 197 ("law is but an act of the will: hence the natural law is divine positive law, and the basis of the goodness and rightness of certain actions is not found in their conformity with nature, but in the absolute will of God").

[142] *Id.* at 65.

[143] Commission Théologique Internationale, *supra note* 15, at 28.

Christian theologians ... acknowledged reason and nature in their interrelation as the universally valid source of law. This step had already been taken by Saint Paul in the Letter to the Romans when he said: 'When Gentiles who have not the Law [the Torah of Israel] do by nature what the law requires, they are a law to themselves ... they show that what the law requires is written on their hearts, while their conscience also bears witness ...' (Rom 2:14f.). Here we see the two fundamental concepts of nature and conscience.[144]

As expounded by Spanish Scholastics, the Catholic doctrine of natural law contains three basic ideas that are essential for understanding the original, or traditional, concept of natural law: (a) the notion of an eternal or divine law, that is, of a "personal God as Lawgiver in the absolute sense;"[145] (b) the idea of man as a blend of matter and soul and the transcendence of the soul; and (c) the idea of the Catholic Church as the supreme earthly interpreter in matters of faith and morals "above the will of the state,"[146] which arises from its mission as a vessel for salvation of souls.

At the core of traditional natural law is the understanding of the "fallen nature" of man, also called the "doctrine of original sin". That is to say, that as a reasonable being with a preternatural disposition, man was created naturally good and with free will to choose from good and evil. The misuse of his freedom caused man to break away from the Eternal God, but even in his fallen state, he is "still able fully to recognize the first principles of morality and law".[147] In that sense, the State and the law are institutional *mediums* conducive to bringing order and justice to a fallen humanity. These institutions are not inherently good or evil, but a *medium*, a tool, to bring man once more in accordance with nature, that is, with God.

Hence, the stark difference between the Scholastic notion of natural law and the ethereal idea of a far-away God propounded by scholars such as Plato, or by the abstract Aristotelian concept of the divine.[148] Such notions contrast the Christian idea of a God incarnate who enters history and forever acquires a personal dimension from the perspective of each individual. Despite the dichotomy created by this pivotal difference, the Fathers of the Church recognized as veritable the attributes ascribed by the ancient

---

144   Reichstag Speech, *supra note* 29.

145   Rommen, *supra note* 9, at 34.

146   *Id.* at 34.

147   *Id.* at 36.

148   *Id.* at 37.

Greeks to the Eternal God as "supreme reason, unchangeable being and omnipotent will".[149] The innovation obviously came to reside in the *personalness* of a former distant God who is now understood to have instilled in the heart of man "a rational and free being".[150] As a result, the evil found at the personal and collective (societal) levels is no longer caused by bad positive law but rather by the intrinsic evilness of the acts themselves. As such, a positive law that calls for or allows an evil act to happen necessarily violates what is natural to man.

6. *The Late Spanish Scholastics*

Natural Law reached its apex in the writings of the Late Spanish Scholastics Vittoria, Bellarmine, Suárez, Vásquez, and De Soto.[151] These writers reaffirmed the "conviction of unalterable principles of morality and law".[152]

The following are the core ideas of the late Spanish Scholastics concerning natural law:

(a) *Natural moral law is immutable as it is the impression of the eternal law in the rational nature of man, "which in turn is an image of God;"*[153]

(b) *It is possible to know "the nature of things, of objective values;"*[154]

(c) It is possible to ascertain the "intrinsic immorality and unlawfulness of certain actions;"[155]

(d) Every action is morally correct only when performed in accordance with "the supreme moral principles that are apprehended by man from nature;"[156]

(e) There exists, as a matter of principle, a "primacy of the intellect over the will".[157] The essence of the law is, consequently, the intellect (or

---

[149] *Id.* at 38.

[150] *Id.*

[151] *Id.* at 40.

[152] *Id.* at 41.

[153] *Id.* at 43.

[154] *Id.* at 41.

[155] *Id.* at 42.

[156] *Id.* at 43.

[157] *Id.* at 62.

reason) and not simply the will. The foundation of the law is not the will of the sovereign, but the intrinsic reasonableness (or intellect) of the law. Therefore, not everything that the sovereign wills can be said to be law, but only what is reasonable, and what is reasonable is what accords to natural law, for to "act in accord with reason and nature is also God's will".[158]

(f)   There is no separation between natural law and the eternal law, because the former is but the reflection of the latter in the human mind (or intellect). Therefore, man is bound to obey certain actions or to refrain from performing them, not because the law states it, but because the law states what is prescribed by the natural law. In that sense, the law (positive, human law) derives its legitimacy from its accordance to the natural law.

(g)   Only the institutions of marriage, property, and contract belong to natural law, but "not the particular prescriptions about marriage and the family, possession and the form of private ownership, and the like".[159]

(h)   The great achievement of the Late Scholastics is the notion that the *ius gentium* "is not *ius naturale*".[160] *Ius gentium*, together with international private law, applies to all peoples at all times, and in that sense, these disciplines are "closely related to the natural law".[161] In other words, the right of war and peace, international trade, contracts, family, inheritance, property, etc., apply indistinctively to all the members of the human race based on natural law.[162]

i)   Marriage between a man and a woman is of divine design and may not be amended or perverted by positive law.[163]

---

[158]   *Id.* at 64.

[159]   *Id.* at 73.

[160]   *Id.* at 68.

[161]   *Id.* at 69.

[162]   *Id.*

[163]   *Id.* at 204 ("[T]he English Parliament is in theory sovereign: it can, to quote an expression which has become almost proverbial, 'do everything but make a woman a man, and a man a woman'").

CHAPTER II:

RE-FOUNDATIONAL ATTEMPTS AGAINST TRADITIONAL NATURAL LAW

1. *Hugo Grotius (1583-1645)*

As already explained, the Scholastics had "cleansed" civil Roman law of its un-Christian elements, and systematized the bulk of what constitutes "traditional natural law". In general terms, the Dutch Hugo Grotius –a rationalist[1]– was perhaps the first writer of prestige to propose a systematic distortion of traditional natural law. In effect, his masterpiece *De iure belli ac pacis* (1625) presented a systematic view of natural law that, overall, agreed with many of the notions advanced by the Scholastics and thus validated them.[2] However, the devil was, as always, in the details.

Grotius proposed that natural law was a discipline *different* from civil law. The key element to understanding this separation is to internalize the notion of *differentness* –not of *separateness*– present at the core of Grotius' explanations. Grotius sustained, like the Scholastics, that natural law and civil law were not only *separate* disciplines, but *different*. And, this distinction constitutes the very source of the decline in the correct understanding of traditional natural law witnessed mainly from the seventeenth century onwards.

By denying a connection of similarity between natural law and civil law, Grotius diminished the correlation between Roman (which was the European "civil" law of his day) and natural law. In reality, what he taught was that Roman law was no longer a product or reason, or at least

---

[1]   *Id.* at 73.

[2]   *Id.* at 71 (For example, Grotius correctly defined the "law of nature" [*ius naturale*] as "a dictate of right reason which points out that an act, according as it is or is not in conformity with rational [and social] nature, has in it a quality of moral baseness or moral necessity; and that, in consequence, such an act is either for-bidden or enjoined by the author of nature, God").

the only product of reason (*ratio scripta*) as it had been known throughout the millennia, even after the Christianization of the Roman Empire.

Grotius' goal was to diffuse or eliminate the ultimate authority of Christianized Roman law as *the* authority in law and to replace it with the new-found conviction that reason –whether or not embodied in Roman law– was the true source of authority and legitimacy (the natural law foundation) of all legal systems. Thus, in Grotius' view, the elements of positive (civil) law were not susceptible to systematic treatment since they often undergo change and are relative.[3] Thus, Grotius opened up the possibility of a drastic reform of private law based on what he called "reason," not Roman law. By detaching "Roman" law from reason, he relativized positive law *and* natural law. This detachment further removed the Protestant European peoples from the Roman law legacy and reformulated their legal systems based on their own understanding of the "law of reason". In a nutshell, though brilliant, Grotius' contribution served to relativize the notion of natural law, in drastic opposition to the teaching of traditional natural law authors.

2. *Natural Law in the Era of Modern Rationalism-Humanism*

Grotius paved the road for the further misconceptions of natural law brought about during the era of rationalism and humanism, also called the "Enlightenment". This philosophical movement –which was essentially "an affair of the ruling class, the nobility and the intellectuals of the age"[4] –sought to liberate natural law "from the fancies and verbiage of the Scholastics".[5] In essence, the Enlightenment was a force of rejection– a Protestant energy[6] unleashed over Europe with eloquent ardor.

The Enlightenment was, inherently, a call to absolutisms; indeed, it proposed final and indubitable conceptions about life and death, about the practical and theoretical sciences, and about natural and positive law. It arrogated to itself the right to regulate the whole spectrum of human life and society regardless of the prescriptions of traditional natural law, to-

---

[3]   Watson, *supra note* 79, at 83-98.

[4]   Rommen, *supra note* 9, at 78.

[5]   *Id.* at 93.

[6]   Edmund Burke, *Letters on the Affairs of Ireland* (1797), *in* Rogers, *supra note* 18, at 462 (referring to the contact of Catholics with Jacobin Protestants in Ireland Burke stated, "whenever their situation brings them nearer into contact with the Jacobin Protestants, they are more or less infected with their doctrines").

ward which it exhibited an exceptional disgust. Instead, the Enlightenment proposed its own "secularist theory of ethics and politics"[7] that came to form the kernel of its "natural-law philosophy".[8] Once the Enlightenment obtained political power, it quickly substituted rational absolutism for monarchical absolutism.

As is broadly known, the Enlightenment used codification as the instrument with which to produce a uniform society under the new reformulation of the natural law that it propagated. This new version of natural law was the byproduct of the "comprehensive moral philosophy of deism,"[9] which was completely separated from the eternal law.[10]

As this new deformation of natural law was based on denials, *e.g.*, a rejection of the existence of absolutes (eternal truths), the Protestant "contractual form" emerged as the essence of societal organization.[11] In other words, the Protestant idea that truth is exclusively what men agree upon permeated the view of natural law as a product of contractual dealings. Political and societal order became, thus, "the product of contracts".[12] The pivotal enlightened contractual form even reached millenary institutions, such as marriage. With marriage, the Enlightenment proposed that if man was able to enter into marriage freely, he was equally free to exit from it. And, as the world terrifyingly witnessed during World War II, man was equally empowered to "contractually" decide when life commenced and ended.

In sum, during the Enlightenment, the State grounded itself on a deformed view of "natural law", which emerged as "the utilitarian product of individual self-interest, cloaked in the solemn and venerable language of the traditional philosophy of natural law".[13]

---

[7]   Rommen, *supra note* 9, at 79.

[8]   *Id.* at 98.

[9]   *Id.* at 80.

[10]   Commission Théologique Internationale, *supra note* 16, at 32 (alluding to modern rationalism, in which "[L]a référence à Dieu devient donc optionnelle. La loi naturelle s'imposerait à tous «même si Dieu n'existait pas (*etsi Deus non daretur*)"— "The reference to God become thus optional. Natural law would impose itself to all, 'even if God did not exist'").

[11]   Rommen, *supra note* 9, at 84 ("[c]ontract affords the sole possible basis of rights").

[12]   *Id.* at 89.

[13]   *Id.*

A. *Samuel von Pufendorf (1632-1694)*

The humanist/rationalist era began with Samuel von Pufendorf[14] and centered itself in an undeterred and absolute reliance on "reason". Pufendorf understood his idea of "reason", in *opposition* to faith, not *complementary* to faith as the traditional natural law had taught during the preceding Christian millennia. Pufendorf's assault on Christian reason carried with it a rejection of all things mystical, categorizing them as possessing an inferior category in the realm of thinking.

Pufendorf's pivotal philosophical idea was that man was "not essentially social,"[15] but an isolated individual in the 'state of nature.'[16] Therefore, social institutions such as marriage, family, inheritance, property, procedural law, constitutional law, the State, and the international community, were not "natural" to man, but simply represented "imperfect"[17] artificial realities. Even though Pufendorf held –like Locke– an optimistic view of the 'state of nature'[18] he apparently never came to know or understand the "doctrine of the eternal law".[19] Through his identification of natural law with eternal law, "human nature [became the] source of natural law".[20] In the end, Pufendorf fell into the same trap of relativizing the hitherto universal notion of traditional natural law.

As will be reviewed later, the doctrine of the state of nature began to make strong inroads into the writings of the Enlightenment philosophers by the middle of the seventeenth century. Their writings so transformed the theory in the cornerstone of the whole rationalist/humanist philosophical movement by the end of that century.[21]

B. *Baruch Spinoza (1632-1677)*

A contemporary assail on traditional natural law occurred in the mid-16th century at the plume of Baruch Spinoza. This philosopher was per-

---

[14]   *Id.* at 75.

[15]   *Id.* at 94.

[16]   *Id.*

[17]   *Id.* at 77.

[18]   *Id.* at 95 ("[t]he law of the state of nature is an ideal law, a model law").

[19]   *Id.* at 97.

[20]   *Id.*

[21]   *Id.* at 76.

haps the first amongst his enlightened colleagues to utterly deny the power of reason in man. He famously declared that "[h]uman nature is at bottom governed by the passions and not by reason".[22] Where the Scholastics had seen goodness and right, Spinoza saw disorder and evil.

Spinoza's materialistic philosophy centered round a few ideas: (a) "might is right:"[23] power determines what is just; (b) disorder and evil are "natural" to man and society; (c) the government is the one institution that brings order, freedom, and prosperity to society; (d) the sovereign's will is the only legitimate law and "demands as a price strict obedience and subordination through identification of natural law with positive law;"[24] (e) positive law is justice and justice is positive law-being and oughtness are but one same thing; and (f) the State occupies the place of omnipresence and omnipotence that traditional natural law had formerly recognized to God alone.

In this way, the siege of traditional natural law under the humanists/rationalists was consummated. In their view, pure human reason —not divine law— was regarded as the foundation of natural law as well as the ultimate source of law. Since human reason was the ultimate legislator, and in this scheme of things positive law is determined by transient legislative majorities, the idea of natural law "thus degenerated from an objective metaphysical idea into a political theory".[25]

Edmund Burke later cautioned against this coup towards traditional natural law:

> ... if no supreme ruler exists, wise to form, and potent to enforce, the moral law, there is no sanction to any contract, virtual or even actual, against the will of prevalent power.[26]

In sum, the differences between the traditional natural law and the "natural rights" theories of the enlightened *philosophes* could be summarized in three: (a) the separation of eternal law and natural moral law; (b) the

---

[22] *Id.* at 85.

[23] *Id.*

[24] *Id.* at 86.

[25] *Id.* at 90.

[26] Edmund Burke, An Appeal from the New to the Old Whigs in Consequence of Some Late Discussions in Parliament, Relative to the Reflections on the French Revolution (1791), in Rogers, supra note 18, at 522.

individualistic approach to the 'state of nature' doctrine; and (c) the "resultant doctrine of the autonomy of human reason".[27]

3. *The Surge of Utilitarianism*

A. *Christian Thomasius (1655-1728)*

Echoing the ancient Epicureans, Christian Thomasius proposed his utilitarian ideology in these terms, "[w]hatever renders the life of men long and happy is to be done, but whatever makes life unhappy and hastens death is to be avoided".[28] He advanced the contorted idea that the temporal "happiness of the individual" is the source of natural law.[29] Happiness was to be understood as a "pleasant, carefree life ... attainable only through a virtuous, respectable, and just life".[30] He combined rights and wrongs, which created the appearance of the truth of the whole.

In fact, under Thomasius' philosophy, there is a total separation of law, morality, and ethics (love, gratitude and reverence).[31] While legal duties are only enforceable externally, moral duties remain in the conscience of the individual. The influence of Protestant Calvinism[32] is clearly perceivable here, with its overwhelmingly individualistic taint.

B. *David Hume (1711-1776)*

Hume went a step further in denying the existence of human reason. In fact, he held reason to be "the slave of the passions",[33] and that passions constitute the "nature" of man. Therefore, Hume proposed, moral principles are not and cannot be based on reason[34] because reason is subordinat-

---

[27]   Rommen, supra note 9, at 93.

[28]   *Id.* at 98.

[29]   *Id.*

[30]   *Id.*

[31]   *Id.* at 121.

[32]   Burke, *Letters on the Affairs of Ireland, supra note* 170, at 463 (defining Protestantism as "a negative religion, –such is the protestant without a certain creed"–).

[33]   Rommen, supra note 9, at 112.

[34]   *Id.* at 113 ("[t]he moral law has no basis in the intelligible rational and social nature of man").

ed to passions. The morality of an action is simply "determined by sentiment;"[35] that is, by its approval or disapproval based on pleasure.

Hume's theory proposed that if an action is approved by the sentiments, it is useful (utilitarian) and accords to morality. As law has to abide by morality, then law must accept what is utilitarian and reject what is not utilitarian, *i.e.*, what does not cause pleasure. On a larger scale, morality is simply the product of a more or less extended social convention. In sum, "good and the just are what is here and now deemed useful to the self-interest of individuals and to their life in common".[36]

C. *Jeremy Bentham (1748-1832)*

The political theory of Jeremy Bentham –who was a declared and consistent adversary of the American independence movement[37]– rests upon one single idea: the principle of utility. With this notion, he aimed at destroying the doctrine of traditional natural law.[38]

To better understand the implications of this theoretical edifice, previous reference must be made to one of the most prominent fathers of British common law, William Blackstone (1723-1780). In Blackstone's exposition of natural law, human laws derive their validity from "the law of nature".[39] Bentham condemned Blackstone,[40] and instead argued that an alleged "natural law" based on tradition was nothing more than an attempt of the "dead to chain down the living".[41] Bentham further proposed that when human laws accord to natural law they "promote happiness".[42] As a result, "this was proof that [natural law] was 'a part of the law of nature".[43] He rejected the right of rebellion against an unjust law –just as Aquinas had proposed in the thirteenth century and Blackstone in the

---

[35]   *Id.* at 112.

[36]   *Id.* at 113.

[37]   Philip Schofield, Utility and Democracy. The Political Thought of Jeremy Bentham (Oxford U. Press, 2006), at 57.

[38]   *Id.* 53.

[39]   *Id.* (quoting Blackstone, "[T]he law of nature was the will of God, and consisted in 'the eternal, immutable laws of good and evil" and following the writings of Thomas of Aquinas).

[40]   *Id.* at 54.

[41]   *Id.* at 61.

[42]   *Id.* at 53.

[43]   *Id.*

eighteenth. Bentham called the right to insurrection "a dangerous maxim",[44] which produced "anarchical tendencies",[45] and that "in justifying the demolition of existing authorities [will] undermine all future ones".[46]

Bentham's ultimate argument was that there was no such thing as "natural law" or "law of nature" or "natural rights"[47] with the power to invalidate positive law. To admit otherwise would –in his words– imply that "[n]o sort of government could survive in these circumstances".[48] It follows that Bentham's exposition of the anti-natural law principle of utility was the notion of the absolute unchecked power of the legislative branch.[49]

Instead of natural law ideas, the principle of utility –or "maximum happiness"– contained the only parameter to measure the validity of positive law.[50]

Ultimately, Bentham's negligible lasting influence is a testament to the nugatory character of his scattered ideas, which he seldom kept uniform throughout his troubled existence.[51]

D. *Thomas Paine (1737-1809)*

Any serious consideration of Tom Paine's ideas is hindered by President Theodore Roosevelt's characterization of Paine as a "filthy little atheist".[52]

---

[44] *Id.* at 54.

[45] *Id.* at 63.

[46] *Id.* at 64.

[47] *Id.* at 68 ("[N]atural rights is simple nonsense: natural and imprescriptible rights, rhetorical nonsense, nonsense upon stilts").

[48] *Id.* at 54.

[49] *Id.* at 57 ("Bentham argued that it was unwise at any time to impose restraints of any kind on a legislature").

[50] *Id.* at 54, 76 ("Talk of utility, and of pains and pleasures, this is grounding your doctrine on matter of fact").

[51] *Id.* at 74 ("[B]y 1822 there did appear to be a greater latitude in Bentham's approach to declarations of rights compared with his position in 1795").

[52] Perry Miller, *Thomas Paine: Rationalist, in* Ray B. Browne. *The Burke-Paine Controversy*: Texts and Criticisms (1963), at 176. *See* Vernon L. Parrington, *Tom Paine: Republican Pamphleteer, in* Ray B. Browne. *The Burke-Paine Controversy*: Texts and Criticisms (1963), at 160(noting that Paine was of Quaker training); *see also* Howard Penniman, *Thomas Paine: Democrat, in* Ray B. Browne. *The Burke-Paine Controversy*: Texts and Criticisms (1963), at 170 (citing Paine's unabashed anti-Christian stance and

Paine was also criticized by his peers due to the systematic absence of *decorum* in his literary style,[53] and his recurrent use of "vulgar phraseology".[54] However, for the sake of completeness, a genuine effort must be undertaken to peruse –even if summarily– the true reach of Paine's approaches to (or rejection of) the natural law doctrine and its misbegotten: the theory of natural rights.

Contrary to Bentham, Paine's philosophy was based on the "natural-rights theory".[55] While the former denied all validity to Tradition (remember his reference to the dead chaining the living), the latter proposed a conditional acceptance of "ancestral arrangements ... only to the extent that they are acceptable to the living".[56] In a sense, Paine was a consummate majoritarianist since he "believed fully in popular sovereignty,"[57] and situated all legitimacy of positive law on the will of the majority.[58] Paine –who was Edmund Burke's longtime intellectual opponent and largely inferior to his rival in the ranks of thinking[59]– also shared a genuine aversion to government, as did other thinkers of his age.[60]

To his merit, Paine held some views which were in tune with the objective principles proposed by traditional natural law. He argued that "equality springs from ultimate principles or natural law,"[61] and that "every child born into the world must be considered as deriving its existence from God".[62]

---

commenting on "his approval of the French revolutionaries' revanchist actions against the Catholic Church").

[53] James T. Boulton, *Tom Paine and the Vulgar Style, in* Ray B. Browne. *The Burke-Paine Controversy*: Texts and Criticisms (1963), at 221 ("[B]y normal standards his writing must be rated low").

[54] *Id.* at 216.

[55] Parrington, *supra note*, at 156.

[56] *Id.* Bentham shared with Paine a sort of intellectual fickleness since in more than one occasion he chastised natural law proponents as advancing the "vanity and presumption of governing beyond the grave."

[57] Penniman, *supra note*, at 170-1.

[58] Parrington, *supra note* 218, at 156 ("there can be no law superior to this popular will expressed through the majority"). *See also* Penniman, *supra note* 219, at 174 ("...he [Paine] assumed that the legislature in a democracy would be supreme").

[59] Miller, *supra note* 220, at 177 ("[I]t was Burke and not Paine who predicted Napoleon").

[60] Boulton, *supra note* 221, at 215 ("man, were he not corrupted by Governments, is naturally the friend of man").

[61] Penniman, *supra note* 219, at 173.

[62] *Id.*

4. *Positivism*

A. *Immanuel Kant (1724-1804)*

Contrary to David Hume, but short of the Scholastics' vein, Kant held that reason was the superior governing power of man and knowledge.[63] Kant's individualistic philosophy sustained that the individual was the radical center of natural law. He deepened the separation between legality and morality. Indeed, he affirmed that, "[t]he motive of juridical legislation is not morality but the keeping of external freedom".[64]

Kant reaffirmed the drastic separation between eternal law and what he called the "rational moral law".[65] For him, "[t]he inherently immoral character of an action is no longer of importance".[66] In this form, he denied the existence of the essence of things by attributing to man the power to define such essence. In this way, for example, marriage becomes "the union of two persons of different sex for life-long reciprocal possession of their sexual faculties".[67] Thus, varying drastically from traditional natural law which taught that marriage was an institution of divine origin created to fulfill the inner goals of humankind-survival, perpetuation, and salvation.

Eventually, Kant proposed that, "the whole body of concrete civil laws (the laws concerning debt, property, the family, and inheritance, in particular the modes of acquiring ownership, conveyance by will and succession, the monetary system and contracts involving monetary considerations) ... became natural law".[68] Kant wholeheartedly adhered to the contractualist view of the State, which for him was "an institution resting on a free contract".[69]

---

[63] Rommen, *supra note* 10, at 87.

[64] *Id.* at 101.

[65] *Id.* at 102.

[66] *Id.* at 103.

[67] *Id.* at 104.

[68] *Id.* at 105.

[69] *Id.*

CHAPTER III:

THE POST-ENLIGHTENMENT
VIEW OF NATURAL LAW

The Enlightenment phraseology broadly utilized and circulated concepts such as: "[n]ature, state of nature, natural reason, natural theology, and natural ethics".[1] The natural law doctrine of the Enlightenment pretended to offer an explanation to all legal categories. Enlightenment scholars regarded the political community "as a mere product of legal conveyances".[2] Other grandiloquently broad concepts utilized by the Enlightenment were the ideals of "civil liberty and equality, [of] economic freedom as a condition of social harmony, and liberation from the rigid bonds of guild law and corporations".[3]

The "individualist natural law of rationalism"[4] strove to demolish traditional natural law by substituting its moralizing philosophy for the Church's traditional teaching. The irony lies in the fact that from the seventeenth century onwards the degenerated enlightened recast of the traditional natural law "passed in the scientific world for the natural law *par excellence*".[5] In a sense, positivism had already triumphed at the turn of the twentieth century when "[m]ost university professors and most practical jurists ... spoke of natural law as a dead letter".[6] However, the monumental distortion of natural law advocated by the Enlightenment did not go unnoticed and the reason is simple; because, "[T]he question of justice is an ethical question, not a juridical one".[7]

---

[1] *Id.* at 107.

[2] *Id.* at 210.

[3] *Id.* at 106.

[4] *Id.* at 107.

[5] *Id.* at 108.

[6] *Id.* at 133.

[7] *Id.* at 248.

1. *The Historical School*

The historical school reacted violently against the Enlightenment's "individualist natural law"[8] and its colossal abuses. Friedrich Carl von Savigny (1779-1861) proposed an identification of natural and human law.[9] Friedrich Julius Stahl (1802-1861) proposed that it is the human community which freely determines the definition of its own law and establishes what is just and reasonable for its own benefit. The degeneration of traditional natural law reached a new low with Stahl; who held that, "positive law which is contrary to God's law is none the less binding".[10]

For the historical school, eternal law "was not a genuinely binding norm",[11] and "[l]aw is will [*voluntas facit legem*] rather than reason".[12] In this way, the historical school pretended to assert a definitive triumph of positive law over traditional natural law.

2. *Hans Kelsen (1881–1973)*

Kelsen propounded the notion that "every norm must be based on and derived from another, a higher norm, and ... this process cannot go on *ad infinitum*".[13] He proposed "a formal basic norm"[14] as a "mere hypothetical construct",[15] which his agnosticism impeded him from calling it "natural law". In turn, Kelsen's "atheistic relativism prevent[ed] him from acknowledging ... a supreme omnipotent will of God as the source of all norms".[16]

Kelsen's biggest mistake was to consider that man is only pure reason.[17] However, his most celebrated achievement amongst the followers of 'natural rights' theory was the identification of "an unbridgeable gulf ... be-

---

[8] *Id.* at 116.

[9] *See id* ("[t]he spirit of the people is the source of human or natural law").

[10] *Id.* at 119.

[11] *Id.*

[12] *Id.*

[13] *Id.* at 146.

[14] *Id.*

[15] *Id.* at 147.

[16] *Id.* at 163.

[17] *Id.* at 177.

tween 'is' and 'ought'".[18] In his positivist understanding, there is no ethical correlation between nature and reason.[19] Nature is "purely functional [and] is incapable of producing any bridge to ethics and law".[20]

In Kelsen's view the same disconnect between nature and law affects reason, and therefore, nothing that is not "verifiable or falsifiable ... belong[s] to the realm of reason .... Hence ethics and religion must be assigned to the subjective field".[21] In sum, as Pope Benedict XVI explains, "[w]here positivist reason dominates the field to the exclusion of all else ... then the classical sources of knowledge for ethics and law are excluded".[22]

Contemporaneous Western societies have embraced Kelsen's legal positivism theory with the fervor of religion.[23] Indeed, the entrenchment of legal positivism has created its own culture, banishing "other cultural realities to the status of subcultures".[24]

In reality, positivist reason with its self-proclaimed exclusivity[25] "recognizes nothing beyond mere functionality"[26] and in fact "diminishes man [and] threatens his humanity".[27]

3. *Materialist Positivism and Modern Totalitarianism*

The assertion that the distortion of traditional natural law favored the development and expansion of ideologies contrary to human dignity after the Enlightenment is not far-fetched. In fact, materialism and positivism served as the juridical *substratum* for the nefarious ideologies of Communism, Fascism, and Nazism during the twentieth century. The washing away of traditional natural law concepts from all spheres of society served as the common kernel of materialism and positivism. Just by way of ex-

---

[18]   Reichstag Speech, supra note 29.

[19]   *Id.*

[20]   *Id.*

[21]   *Id.*

[22]   *Id.*

[23]   *Id.* (alluding to the fact that in Europe "there are concerted efforts to recognize only positivism as a common culture and a common basis for law-making").

[24]   *Id.*

[25]   *Id.*

[26]   *Id.*

[27]   *Id.*

ample, "[t]he two countries where juridical and moral positivism had obtained a dominant position in the universities, in the legal profession, and in the official philosophies of law",[28] namely, Germany and Italy, were the stages where Nazism and Fascism flourished.

The materialist deification of legal positivism denied essential concepts of traditional natural law; including, the existence of an eternal law, eternal justice, free will, an unalterable moral law, the complex composition of man as a welter of matter and soul, the transcendent origin and destiny of man, the haughtiness of human dignity, and the necessary limitations over the whole human power and government. The idea that "[p]ositive law alone exists"[29] and that law "is merely a creation of the state"[30] denied the existence of a moral backbone to the whole human phenomenon. New slanted dogmas built over the ashes of traditional natural law were adopted after the Enlightenment and reached their apex during the apogee of the inhuman doctrines that half destroyed humanity in the twentieth century. Amongst these twisted ideas, the deification of the State as the "creator of morality and law"[31] and source of "the highest goods that man possesses–freedom, property, family, personal rights"[32] wreaked havoc. The deification of the State was the *necessary result* of the reduction of man[33] and unleashed unprecedented terror and destruction in the Western world during the twentieth century.

In effect, the will of the State with its monopoly of political power and force, was regarded as the law. Consequently, the "[law] is neither reason nor will [but] real force",[34] and "a totalitarian regime, can declare anything law".[35] This absolutist view was "even greater than that of the absolute monarch ... who considered himself bound by the natural and divine law".[36] Under the materialistic philosophy, the term 'natural' underwent

---

[28]   Rommen, supra note 9, at 152.

[29]   *Id.* at 127.

[30]   *Id.*

[31]   *Id.*

[32]   *Id.*

[33]   *Id.* at 131 ("man exists as a *datum* prior to all positive law").

[34]   *Id.* at 128.

[35]   *Id.* at 156.

[36]   *Id.* at 128.

"an even more wanton disfigurement than it suffered at the hands of Hobbes, Hume, or the utilitarians".[37]

However, the extremes to which materialist positivism and modern totalitarianism traversed to "opened the eyes of more and more thinking people to the ultimate consequences to which the denial of the natural law must lead".[38]

---

[37] *Id.* at 154.

[38] *Id.* at 155.

CHAPTER IV:

THE RETURN TO TRADITIONAL NATURAL LAW IN THE 19TH CENTURY

Traditional natural law has ever remarkably, and for the sake of humanity, made an impressive come back since the era when the Enlightenment proclaimed its demise. However, a mere denial of the unreasonableness of positivism was not going to "lead straight to the idea of natural law".[1] A more coherent presentation and *aggiornamento* [update] of the traditional natural law had to come, and it first did in the writings of several Catholic authors since the late eighteenth century.

1. *Antonio Rosmini Serbati (1797–1855)*

This great philosopher of law was born in the late eighteenth century and his works remain largely not translated from the original Italian they were written in. Rosmini's masterpiece titled *Filosofia dil Diritto* [Philosophy of Law] contained a fresh take on the most important topics of natural law. A few references to the key concepts developed by him are included below.

Sensitive to the fact that the philosophical bankruptcy of the Enlightenment had given birth to widespread unbelief in the Old Continent, Rosmini maturely asserted that nothing good could come from the philosophy of skepticism or indifferentism.[2] Skeptics, in the first place —he retorted— are themselves convinced of not having anything for certain and, consequently, remain devoid of any clear principle or criterion with which to regulate their judgment or issue a judicial decision. The logical result is that those who in theory or in practice profess skepticism, however many there are in the world, may not "judge the truth and the moral value of a

---

[1]   *Id.* at 145.

[2]   Antonio Rosmini, *Filosofia del Diritto* (Padova, Cedam-Casa Editrice Dott. Antonio Milani, 1967), Vol. 35, at 223.

given religion".[3] The lack of a firm persuasion of those who do not believe that they undoubtedly possess the truth, renders them unable to judge those who do have such solid persuasions.

Rosmini also noticed that the replacing of solid moral ground with "sensible utility" was the great principle of the skeptical movement during the transition from the Middle Ages to the modern era. He discovered that this same practical criterion was to be found at the root of the decadence of Greece and then Rome.[4] The skeptical approach denied man the power to know the truth. This view desired that man direct himself in accordance with the "utility" proven by experience. However, as Rosmini explained, this same "utility" differs from true opinion in that it lacks a general practical criterion for its determination.[5] If skeptical men were to judge cases involving believing men, they would have to judge according to the religious beliefs of the believing, or otherwise abstain from judging them. In sum, Rosmini teaches that skeptical men do not have the right to judge the veracity or the morality of the religion that most men profess because their own beliefs are uncertain and vacillating.

Now, concerning those who showed "indifference toward religion," in our author's view they consider all religions to be the same, that is, equally uncertain. In this way, these men place all religions at the same level of uncertainty. Skeptics preach that, "it should be considered as temerarious to refer to one's own religion in absolute terms".[6] In this state of things, the search for truth, therefore, becomes a work of mere conjectures, developed according to the principle of utilitarianism, or depending on the feeling or taste that each one has toward this or that belief. The conjecture of each individual –indifferentism suggests– must be respected as much as the conjecture of any other person.

The philosophical approaches of skepticism and indifferentism truly found their common expression in the doctrine of freedom of conscience. In this sense, the ultimate goal of finding a universal truth valid, in every time and place, becomes purposeless, and the quest for universal truth is abandoned for subjective particularities.[7] In contrast to these false philos-

---

[3] *Id.* at 224.

[4] Edmund Burke, *An Abridgment of English History* (1757), *in* Rogers, *supra note* 16, at 551 (stating that, "[f]rom Rome the whole western world had received its Christianity").

[5] Rosmini, *supra* note 278, 224.

[6] *Id.*

[7] *Id.*

ophies, Rosmini proposed the philosophies of true religion and true morality. These philosophies present responses valid to every man in every *époque* and location because they are precisely based on the nature of man. In sum, and once again, Rosmini did a remarkable job in striving to explain to his contemporaries the essence of the invariable discipline of traditional natural law.

2. *Pope Pius IX*

Well into the nineteenth century, the human and political consequences of the natural law ideology born out of the Enlightenment –or rather the distortion of traditional natural law– had already begun to appear in the Western world. But not all voices were silent. In fact, Pope Pius IX in his Syllabus of 1864 proclaimed several propositions:

(a) "[m]oral laws do not require a divine sanction, nor is there any need for human laws to be conformable to the law of nature or to receive their binding force from God;" (b) "[r]ights consist in the mere material fact, and all human duties are an empty name, and every human deed has the force of right;" and (c) "[t]he commonwealth is the origin and source of all rights, and enjoys rights which are not circumscribed by any limits".[8]

With these statements, an author has rightly remarked that:

the resistance which Catholicism has offered to totalitarianism and its pseudoreligious political creeds is not based exclusively on dogmatic theology but above all on natural law.[9]

Yet, Nathaniel Micklem, for example, has commented that,

the ... Protestant Church in Germany ... which rejects ... the idea of natural law, has had a less advantageous basis for its resistance to Hitlerism, whereas the Catholics have had the natural-law doctrine to lean on in addition to their religious principles.[10]

---

[8]   Rommen, *supra* note 9, at 122.

[9]   *Id.* at 153.

[10]   *Id.*

3. *Leo XIII*

Pope Leo XIII extensively used the Catholic doctrine of traditional natural law "for constructing Christian social theory".[11] In fact, Leo XIII refers to natural law to identify the source of civil authority and determine its limits. He adds that it is necessary to obey God more than men when there is a conflict between positive (or human) laws and divine or natural laws.[12]

---

[11] *Id.* at 123.

[12] Commission Théologique Internationale, *supra note* 15, at 34.

CHAPTER V:

A CONCEPTUAL REVIEW OF THE SYSTEMATIC DISTORTION OF TRADITIONAL NATURAL LAW AND ITS SUBSTITUTION BY THE "NATURAL RIGHTS" THEORY

1. *A Starting Point: John Locke (1632-1704)*

John Locke is broadly considered as the father of the "natural rights" movement that shacked Europe from the late seventeenth century onwards. Locke's 'natural rights' theory purportedly replaced the traditional natural law doctrine. But in reality, the 'natural law' conceptions of the enlightened philosophers were undoubtedly a rehash of the ancient Greek Sophists' ideas.[1] In any case, John Locke –a self-professed Protestant Anglican[2]– proposed a 'natural rights' theory that had an enormous influence on both sides of the Atlantic. He is considered in some circles as the remote father of U.S. constitutionalism: Thomas Jefferson himself "was accused of copying the Declaration of Independence from Locke's Treatise of Government".[3]

Therefore, in order to understand the main elements of the 'natural rights' theory, it is essential to review Locke's philosophical ideas. His conception of natural law was fundamentally an assertion of the individual against the collectivity. Specifically, Locke's individualistic theory was a "catalogue or bundle of individual rights that stem from individual self-interest".[4] Thus, Locke turned the Tomistic view of the common good against itself when he proclaimed that common good was "nothing real

---

[1]   Rommen, *supra note* 9, at 8.

[2]   Locke, *supra note* 4, at 110 (stating "Bilson, a bishop of our church...").

[3]   Tom Crawford, *in* preamble to Locke, Locke, *supra note* 5, at III.

[4]   Rommen, supra note 9, at 89.

[but] merely the sum of the particular goods or interests of individuals".[5] Yet Locke dared to borrow the Scholastics' linguistic nomenclature and called his ideology 'natural law,' which in his view was merely "a dictate of common sense".[6]

Locke's misleading verbosity was quickly detected by Edmund Burke, also a famous British political thinker.[7] Burke is said to have declared that Locke's *Treatise on Civil Government* "was the worst book ever written".[8] Stylistically, Locke's literary arrogance is easily detected in his *Treatise* by its lack of citations. The most plausible conclusion that can be drawn from these omissions is that perhaps he was breaking with the past, to which he thought he owed nothing. Locke even substituted the notion of the "unwritten"[9] "law of nature"[10] for the traditional natural law.

As will be reviewed later, Locke's mental gymnastics serve as a clever attempt to trick the ignorant, the unaware, or the willing. His admixtures of wrongs with rights make it more difficult to uncover his theoretical background. In him, truly, became flesh the *dictum* of his countryman Hilaire Belloc who, in 1938, stated that, "all heresies [survive] by the Catholic truths which [they] retain".[11]

Accordingly, we will review now both the accurate as well as the distorted philosophical ideas of Locke concerning natural law.

---

[5] *Id.*

[6] *Id.* at 90.

[7] Burke has been reputed a defender of aristocracy. However, his political trajectory and his writings debunk such views ("nobility are as perfectly willing to act the part of flatterers, tale-bearers, parasites, pimps, and buffoons, as any of the lowest and vilest of man-kind can possibly be.)" Edmund Burke, *Speech on Economic Reform* (February 1780), *in* Rogers, *supra note* 18, at 248); *see also* Edmund Burke, *Thought on the Present Discontents* (1770), *in* Rogers, *supra note* 18, at 130 ("I am no friend to aristocracy").

[8] Peter J. Stanlis, *Edmund Burke and the Natural Law* (Transaction Publishers, 2003), at 139 ("[I]n 1793 the Constitutional Society of Sheffield printed an abstract of Locke's Treatise on Civil Government, the preface of which stated: 'Edmund Burke, the Knight Errant of Feudality, declared in the House of Commons, that 'Locke's Treatise on Civil Government, was the worst book ever written'").

[9] Locke, supra note 4, at 63.

[10] *Id.* at 62.

[11] Hilaire Belloc, *The Great Heresies* (The Catholic Book Club, Ed., 1938), at 128.

A. *On Locke's Statements Amicable to Traditional Natural Law*

In fairness to Locke, several of his propositions do bear truth *because* they accord to traditional natural law. Even though he rejected traditional natural law, this discipline formed his intellectual and educational background at Oxford.

For instance, (a) on the sanctity of marriage between a man and a woman, Locke recognizes that, "the end of conjunction between male and female [is] not barely procreation, but the continuation of the species".[12]

(b) With respect to the natural law duty of parents toward children, Locke writes that,

Adam and Eve, and after them all parents, were by the law of nature under an obligation to preserve, nourish, and educate the children they had begotten; not as their own workmanship, but the workmanship of their own Maker.[13]

(c) Concerning the natural necessity of civil society, he writes:

every man who has entered into civil society, and is [*sic*] become a member of any commonwealth, has thereby quitted his power to punish offences against the law of nature in prosecution of his own private judgment, yet with the judgment of offences, which he has given up to the legislative in all cases where he can appeal to the magistrate.[14]

(d) On the exclusion of tyranny and oppression from civil society, he expresses that, "tyranny is the exercise of power beyond right, which nobody can have a right to".[15] Likewise, he follows up with the statement that, "man, not having such an arbitrary power over his own life, cannot give another man such a power over it".[16] In addition, he makes it clear that, "[w]herever law ends tyranny begins".[17]

(e) Finally, with respect to freedom itself, Locke proposes that, "freedom of nature is to be under no other restraint but the law of nature".[18] The same approach goes for the natural law right to religious freedom,

---

[12] Locke, *supra note* 4, at 35.

[13] *Id.* at 25.

[14] *Id.* at 39.

[15] *Id.* at 91.

[16] *Id.* at 79.

[17] *Id.* at 92.

[18] *Id.* at 11.

when he asserts that, "neither Pagan nor Mahometan, nor Jew, ought to be excluded from the civil rights of the commonwealth because of his religion".[19]

2. *The Errors of the "Natural Rights" Theory Exposed*

The "entire revolutionary tradition of 'natural rights' [was] introduced by Hobbes and popularized by Locke".[20] The doctrinal errors of this movement bred by the Enlightenment concerning natural law are legion. We will review them next.

A. *The Abstract Notion of 'Natural Rights'*

The liberal philosophical and political ideology advanced by the Enlightenment was altogether revolutionary, in that it proposed a concept of "natural rights" and "rights of man" in the abstract. This generalization confounded all sorts of citizens "into one homogeneous mass".[21] At the center of this theory was an immaterial idea of bare –and largely unexplained– equality.

Against this proposition of an abstract morality –which even Aristotle had rejected–,[22] Edmund Burke, for instance, highlighted that the "natural rights" theory "sought to provide for all contingencies by utilizing speculative reason and a mathematical foundation and method".[23] In fact, the enlightened *philosophes* utilized "*a priori* laws of mathematical reasoning to create a national constitution centered in an abstract social equality".[24] The Enlightenment rejected the obvious reality that politics is a "practical and not a theoretical science".[25] Furthermore, as Burke pointed out, "men did not behave toward each other simply as men in the abstract, but as

---

[19]   Locke, supra note 40, at 149.

[20]   Stanlis, *supra note* 8, at 23.

[21]   *Id.* at 108.

[22]   Edmund Burke, *Speech on Conciliation With America* (1775), *in* Rogers, *supra note* 18, at 200 ("Aristotle, the great master of reasoning, cautions us and with great weight and propriety, against lb' species of delusive geometrical accuracy in moral arguments, as the most fallacious of all sophistry").

[23]   Stanlis, supra note 8, at 114.

[24]   *Id.* at 94.

[25]   *Id.* at 110.

citizens of a world political commonwealth".[26] In sum, the Enlightenment contradicted the reality that truly "no moral questions are ever abstract questions".[27]

B. *A Scientific Approach to Political Realities*

Jean Jacques Rousseau (1712-1778) had "preached a state of nature that resembled the biblical Paradise".[28] Referring to this and other "vain and deluded sophists ... guilty of a Faustian pride,"[29] Edmund Burke criticized their:

> ... being consumed in endless and futile speculations about the structure of the universe, the meaning of history, the origin and nature of civil society, liberty, justice, and the abstract 'rights of man.'[30]

Contrary to the abstract delusion of the Enlightenment, traditional natural law had taught that all legal or political philosophies and propositions must be rooted in the truth, and that the good or evil consequences produced by them must be carefully assessed before embarking in the implementation of abstract notions. Ultimately, civil society must be governed according to the concrete reason expressed throughout experience and the reason of a "whole people".[31]

C. *An Extreme Concept of Popular Sovereignty*

The French Revolution codified what is perhaps the most important tenet of the Enlightenment philosophy - the principle of popular sovereignty. This principle held that the will of an abstract and undetermined "people" was, without any limitations, the supreme authority in all things concerning self-government. In negative terms, the principle implied that a sovereign people recognized no authority whatsoever above itself.

The principle of popular sovereignty, as explained by the Enlightenment, ran contrary to traditional natural law. In fact, for natural law there

---

[26] *Id.*

[27] Edmund Burke, Speech on a Motion for Leave to Bring in a Bill to Repeal and Alter Certain Acts Respecting Religious Opinions (1792), in Rogers, supra note 18, at 478.

[28] Rommen, supra note 9, at 91.

[29] Stanlis, supra note 8, at 109.

[30] *Id.*

[31] *Id.* at 113.

is no abstract sovereignty of the people.[32] The real sovereignty is the primacy of the positive law *as and when* founded on the natural law instilled in man by God. In other words, the people are not free to agree in whatever they wish. The people may only agree to what is just, true, and good. This is, precisely, the reason why positive law does not find its ultimate support in itself, that is, in popular sovereignty. To be authentic, positive law must find its principle and foundation in the law of God, written in the human mind and heart, and known as natural law.

D. *The Unlimited Supremacy of the Legislative Branch of Government*

A key constitutional principle of the French Revolution was the supremacy of the legislative branch of government.[33] The French Revolution was a cruel experiment of usurpation, robbery, violation of basic human rights,[34] terror,[35] and "confiscations, banishments, imprisonments, and death, decreed in a mass".[36]

E. *A Softened Right of Rebellion*

Before the War of Independence, the original thirteen British colonies in America were already familiar with the principle of the legal supremacy of Parliament.[37] However, this principle was never understood as conferring "*omnipotence* of parliament".[38] In consequence, when the British Par-

---

[32]   Gentz, supra *note 18*, at xvii ("[T]here is also no abstract sovereignty of the people, because the law is above any sovereign except God").

[33]   More on this topic may be reviewed in Figueroa, *supra note* 101.

[34]   *Id.* at 89 (referring to the "presumption of the natural and inevitable hatred, which these crimes [the French Revolution's] must every where rouse against them, was a sufficient ground to them to treat as an offender deserving death, every man, who did not immediately and actively associate with them").

[35]   *Id.* at 87. *See also* Dante Figueroa, *La Revolución Francesa: Una Perspectiva Histórica para Entender su Legado Jurídico en Latinoamérica* [The French Revolution: A Historic Perspective to Understand its Legal Legacy in Latin America], Ars Boni et Aequi (Law Review of the Bernardo O'Higgins University, Santiago, Chile), Volume 7, 2011; Figueroa, *supra note* 100.

[36]   *Id.* at 91.

[37]   Gentz, supra *note* 19, at 41("… the parliament had always exercised the legislative power over the colonies, in every thing which concerned trade, whether of export, or of import…").

[38]   *Id.* at 42.

liament enacted oppressive laws against the American colonies in the eighteenth century, the colonies rightly invoked their natural law right of insurrection against tyranny.[39] In doing so, the American colonies simply invoked a principle of traditional natural law already systematized by Saint Thomas of Aquinas in the thirteenth century. Otherwise, the legal foundation of the American colonies' insurrection against British rule could not be found in positive law.

In effect, extant positive law –both British and colonial– divided the legislative and executive powers "between the king and the provincial assemblies".[40] This imitated the situation in England, where power was split "between the king and the two houses of parliament".[41] Therefore, it was legal (that is, according to positive law) for the King to levy taxes on the American colonies "such as the provincial assemblies proposed".[42] Therefore, when the Tea Act of 1773 was imposed on the American colonies without their consent, [43] the American colonies had to find the legal foundations of their right to rebellion *outside* the existing written legal instruments that governed them. Consequently, in due course, the colonies resorted to the teachings of traditional natural law concerning the right to just rebellion against tyranny. In that sense, the American Revolution was as much a "revolution of necessity"[44] as it was a "defensive revolution".[45] To the great credit of the American colonies, after their independence declaration in 1776, they escaped the "deadly passion for making political experiments with abstract theories, and untried systems,"[46] unlike the French Revolution did a few years later in 1789.

At this point, the wisdom of the Founding Fathers is remarkably illustrated by their "unquestionable aversion ... to the French revolution, and to all what since 1789, has been called revolutionary principles".[47]

---

[39] *Id.* at 43.

[40] *Id.* at 46.

[41] *Id.*

[42] *Id.* at 47.

[43] *Id.* at 48 (demonstrating that since there was not a written Constitution guaranteeing them the right of rebellion (or "legal resistance").

[44] *Id.* at 62.

[45] *Id.* at 66.

[46] *Id.* at 69.

[47] *Id.* at 73.

F. *A Diluted Right to Disobey an Unjust Law*

The great theologian Origen explained, in the third century, the natural law-founded right of resistance against unjust laws in these terms:

> Suppose that a man were living among the Scythians, whose laws are contrary to the divine law, and was compelled to live among them . ... [S]uch a man for the sake of the true law, though illegal among the Scythians, would rightly form associations with like-minded people contrary to the laws of the Scythians.[48]

The doctrine of unjust law is one of the most remarkable principles of traditional natural law and, simply stated, teaches that, "a positive law that commands something which is in itself unjust and immoral must be regarded as non-law".[49] It was Saint Thomas of Aquinas who developed in more detail the doctrine justifying insurrection against an unjust law. In that vein, and centuries after St. Thomas of Aquinas, another Saint (Thomas More), unapologetically sustained that it was "insufficient in law to charge any Christian to obey" a law which contradicted the law given by Christ.[50] His response came based on traditional natural law-that law could not be considered as a law.

John Locke –rightly in this aspect– followed St. Thomas of Aquinas' natural law reasoning on the right of rebellion, and indicated that this was "an opposition, not to persons, but to authority [...] founded only in the constitutions and laws of the government".[51] In effect, Locke added that,

> using force upon the people without authority, and contrary to the trust put in him that does so, is a state of war with the people, who have a right to reinstate their legislative in the exercise of their power ... [the people have]... a right to remove it [the aggressor] by force.[52]

---

[48]   Reichstag Speech, *supra note* 30.

[49]   Rommen, *supra note* 10, at 256.

[50]   Thomas More, The life of Sir Thomas More, Kt. lord high chancellour of England (1726), at 255.

[51]   Locke, *supra note* 5, at 102.

[52]   *Id.* at 71.

Reinstating the traditional natural law of rebellion against an unjust law, Edmund Burke hammered that "[w]hen tyranny is extreme, and abuses of government intolerable, men resort to the rights of nature to shake it off".[53]

G. *The Alleged 'State of Nature': A Concept Foreign to Traditional Natural Law*

The existence of an alleged 'state of nature' was critical to the 'natural rights' theory built by the Enlightenment. In the context of the history of philosophy, that theory was genuinely novel. In fact, the ancient Greeks never worried themselves with such a theoretical construct. Plato (in the *"Laws"*) and Aristotle (in *"Politics"*) conceived the city (*polis*) as the natural human community ruled by the moral law of nature. The idea of 'state of nature' does not find any precedent in the moral law of nature, such as the type taught by Cicero. Comparatively, due to their eminently practical spirit, the Romans never troubled themselves about the notion of a primitive man.

Thomas Hobbes (1588-1679) was the first philosopher to propose the idea of a hypothetical 'state of nature.'[54] In this pretended situation, isolated men were ready to destroy one another. To avoid the disaster threatening the human race, men would have subscribed to a series of contractual acts transferring all of their power and force to a common entity, a one assembly of men alone, called "the State". In this way, men entrusted their security to a common power.

In his *Leviathan* (1651), Hobbes states that:

During the time men live without a common power to keep them all in awe, they are in that condition called war; and such a war, as if of every man, against every man.

In the Hobbian world, the State monopolizes force as a result of the prior transference made by isolated and terrorized individuals who desperately felt the urge to exit from the 'state of nature.' In Hobbes' view, men exited the hellish 'state of nature' by subscribing a social contract with the State to which they transferred all of their power and force.

---

[53] Edmund Burke, *Speech on the Acts of Uniformity* (1772), *in* Rogers, *supra note* 18, at 468.

[54] Roberto Bin & Giovanni Pitruzzella *"Diritto Costituzionale"* [*"Constitutional Law"*] (G. Giappichelli Editore, Torino, 2011), at 16.

Building upon Hobbes' theorizations, Locke systematized the 'state of nature' ideology calling it a "state of perfect freedom to order their [men's] actions and dispose of their possessions ... within the bounds of the law of nature".[55] In this environment, men were "by nature all free, equal, and independent".[56] The objection raised by traditional natural law is that the ideal Lockean situation of freedom and equality was not an ontological argumentation in the realm of being. Instead, it was a situational, historical moment in time. Whether this appreciation came from confusion, manipulation, or tergiversation is not clear.

On the other hand, as evidence of his 'state of nature,' Locke mentions the case of the men of Peru, who "for a long time had neither kings nor commonwealths, but lived in troops".[57] Whether due to conscious tergiversation or sheer ignorance, he did not reveal his awareness that the Incan civilization had not only a king, but a conquering Emperor. His example, therefore, is not only inaccurate, but historically false.

Continuing with Locke's lucubration, in the 'state of nature' "the enjoyment of the property [man] has ... is very unsafe, very unsecure".[58] In consequence, "for the mutual preservation of their lives, liberties, and estates [which he calls in general 'property',]"[59] men would have entered into the social compact.

However, as the master of confusion that he was, Locke justified his dilettanti reasoning on the alleged 'state of nature' by adding sound ideas previously taught by traditional natural law. Locke recognized that the 'state of nature' was subject to a twofold constraint: by "a law of nature" that binds everyone; and by reason, which is the law that "teaches all mankind [that] being all equal and independent, no one ought to harm another in his life, health, liberty, or possessions".[60]

Once again, Locke presented an admixture of truths promoted by traditional natural law and half-truths that distorted the whole edifice of our discipline and the very foundations of Western legal systems.

---

[55]   Locke, *supra note* 4, at 2.

[56]   *Id.* at 44.

[57]   *Id.* at 46.

[58]   *Id.* at 57.

[59]   *Id.*

[60]   *Id.* at 3.

H. *The Religionist Foundation of the 'State of Nature' Theory*

In his *Letter on Toleration*, Locke –a self-appointed political theologian[61]– defined "a church [as a] voluntary society of men, joining themselves together of their own accord in order to the public[ally] worship God [in] a free and voluntary society".[62] Hence, he departed from the millenary established religion of Europe through his denial of two crucial principles: (1) that the Church is of divine origin and not man-made; and (2) that the rule of Apostolic Succession secures the Church's role in the course of human history.

The few theological ideas that shaped Locke's Protestant[63] political philosophy may be summarized as follows: (a) the radical separation between religion and civil government;[64] (b) the rejection of any human mediation between man and God;[65] (c) that religion is a private matter, *ergo*, the government may neither adhere to a official religion nor ban the existence of a particular religion;[66] (d) that social concerns rest outside the purview of the government;[67] and (e) that the primacy of one's own conscience stands above everything else.[68]

In this context, Protestantism is the mother of the 'state of nature' theory. In effect, beginning in the sixteenth century, Calvinism had denied that man's right reason and will had any part in his moral redemption. The Calvinist dogma of the "elect" and the "depraved" made man's salvation depend entirely upon God's grace. The implied political corollary of this dogma was that some men were thought to be born to rule while others

---

[61]   Locke, *supra note* 40, at 122-3. Locke loyally adhered to the political religion established by Henry VIII.

[62]   *Id.* at 120.

[63]   *Id.* at 131 ("[F]aith only, and inward sincerity, are the things that procure acceptance with God").

[64]   *Id.* at 126 ("the church itself is a thing absolutely separate and distinct from the commonwealth").

[65]   *Id.* at 128 ("[T]he care, therefore, of every man's soul belongs unto himself, and is to be left unto himself").

[66]   *Id.* at 124 ("[F]or the civil government can give no new right to the church nor the church to the civil government").

[67]   *Id.* at 133 ("[T]he only business of the church is the salvation of souls, and it no way concerns the commonwealth.").

[68]   *Id.* at 142 ("liberty remains to men in reference to their eternal salvation, and that is, that everyone should do what he in his conscience is persuaded to be acceptable to the Almighty").

were predestined to serve. In this way, the blending of Calvinism and the 'natural rights' theory occurred:

> Between 1660 and 1800 [when] Calvinism became thoroughly impregnated with the rationalistic spirit of natural science, and developed that love of simplicity, which Hobbes and the deists venerated.[69]

Additionally, the Enlightened philosophers advanced the idea that,

> private conscience in religion and natural rights in politics [are] wholly a matter of private reason, and no church or state should come between a man's conscience and God.[70]

Consequently, as human beings in their 'state of nature' were pure, and relied in their own private reason, the "factious passions"[71] which attack man were thought to be the product of civil society. Consequently, the ideal religious goal of man "became deism or pantheism".[72] Deism, which developed alongside Calvinism, strongly objected revealed Christianity and sought to substitute it by a "natural" religion.[73] In fact, deists attacked human institutions, such as the State and government, as "artificial" and "unnatural".[74] Therefore, the deist found a clear antithesis between their 'state of nature' doctrine and the state of 'artificial' society.

The religionist *substratum* of the 'state of nature' theory is further evidenced in the many calls for a return to the "primitive Church of the first four centuries"[75] voiced since the eighteenth century. The religionist assumption was expressed in clear terms,

> established churches necessarily violate men's consciences, and ... the use of liturgy, drama, and aesthetic appeals in worship are 'unnatural' corruptions of Christianity.[76]

Even more boldly stated, an exaltation occurred of the "primitive simplicity and popular sovereignty of the early Church [which] contained the

---

[69] Stanlis, *supra note* 296, at 182.

[70] *Id.* 151.

[71] *Id.* 152.

[72] *Id.* at 158.

[73] *Id.* at 125.

[74] *Id.* (citing Bishop Butler in his 1736 book, *The Analogy of Religion*).

[75] *Id.* at 148 (paraphrasing Joseph Priestly in his 1782 *History of the Corruptions of Christianity*).

[76] *Id.*

only norm for Christianity".[77] This "simplicity" found in the "primitive Christianity of the first three centuries"[78] was accompanied by the ideas of a direct appeal to God or 'nature'[79] and paved the ground for the formulation of the "principle of private or popular sovereignty".[80]

Therefore, behind this iconoclast paradigm a zealous appeal "to a primitive state of nature as a political norm"[81] existed. The political "ideal of simplicity"[82] was thought to be intrinsically united with the law of nature and the idea of 'natural rights.'[83] The return to a simple and 'primitive' Christianity became a political goal, according to which "all men would have equal rights by having an equal share of power".[84] The final religionist proposition at the core of the 'natural rights' theory was that of a revolutionary egalitarianism[85] based on the notion that, "each man derives his civil rights directly from God or 'nature,' rather than indirectly through civil society".[86]

The political expression of this pinnacle of rejection later made its way into the French Assembly, which made an impassionate call for a return to "primitivism" in religion policies and political life.[87] In fact, as many Anglo-revolutionaries proclaimed in the years after the French Revolution, "the French National Assembly, by abolishing the established religion and making everyone free to choose for himself, moved toward the true religious ideal. But it did not go far enough".[88] The French –it was added– "should have ventured to proceed to a total annihilation of their civil establishment in religion".[89]

---

[77] *Id.* at 154 (citing Francis Stone in his 1792 book, *An Examination of Burke's Reflections*).

[78] *Id.* at 158.

[79] *Id.* at 159.

[80] *Id.* at 158.

[81] *Id.* at 148.

[82] *Id.* at 150.

[83] *Id.* at 153 (noting that the "abused and corrupt State ... departed from its original beautiful simplicity, and has superseded those rights, which the God of nature had given to mankind").

[84] *Id.* at 155.

[85] *Id.*

[86] *Id.* at 156.

[87] *Id.* at 133.

[88] *Id.* at 154.

[89] *Id.*

In sum, according to the religionist perspective of the 'state of nature,' government institutions become a hindrance between God and men "preventing them from living according to their original equality in a state of nature".[90] Burke alluded that the hypocrisy of the alleged Lockean "tolerance" in all matters religious and political was "the advocate for the largest scheme of ecclesiastical and civil toleration to Protestants".[91]

The Responses of Traditional Natural Law to the Religionist Views of the 'state of nature'

At the root of the 'state of nature' theory lays a denial of the original sin doctrine.[92] In fact, the belief that there are two types of men –the elected and the depraved– translated into the political theory that man was inherently and naturally good in a former world, called the 'state of nature.' Under the Calvinist belief of universal innate depravity, the elected had been already redeemed and saved from sin by divine grace; while the depraved were accursed since the beginning of times. Consequently, in the Calvinist scheme, there is no space for the complicated doctrine of original sin, according to which the forces of goodness and sin exist in each human being, at all times, and in all circumstances. Thus, political and social institutions reflect this intricate reality of the human phenomenon.

Calvinism's political philosophy was hence transposed into the political arena from the eighteenth century onwards. While Calvinism had an unrelenting trust in grace, deism –the other religionist force behind the 'natural rights' theory– it had a blind reliance on human reason and in man's rational natural benevolence, as explained by the deists.[93]

Against rationalism and sentimentalism, traditional natural law teaches that original sin is at the root of all social problems. Man's "inherent capacity for both good and evil"[94] is "mixed and partial in all".[95] The distin-

---

[90]   *Id.* at 146.

[91]   Edmund Burke, Edmund Burke, *Speech on the Acts of Uniformity* (1772), *in* Rogers, *supra note* 18, at 469 (denying any toleration to Catholics at all).

[92]   Stanlis, *supra note* 296, at 187.

[93]   *Id.* at 182.

[94]   *Id.* at 186.

[95]   *Id.*

guishing attributes of free will and right reason distinguish that those who are lost are those who will their own perdition.[96]

In the traditional view of natural law, evil is "only slightly subordinated to good".[97] In his fallen state –Edmund Burke said– man is "capable, through God's grace and his own right reason and free will" of personal and social redemption.[98]

With respect to the idea of 'reason' proposed by the deists, Burke noticed that this:

> was not the Ciceronian 'right reason' of the classical Natural Law. [but] merely the mathematical logic of natural science applied to moral problems[99]

Burke also considered "primitive" Christianity "a revolutionary delusion,"[100] or a "revolutionary tendency of the state of nature theory [aimed at destroying] the established order".[101]

In definitive, the 'natural rights' philosophical wanderings ignored reality and all natural human differences since "the worst possible civil society was superior to any hypothetical simple 'state of nature.'[102]

I. *The Idea of 'State of Nature' is Based on An Erroneous Conception of Human Nature*

Thomas Hobbes proposed a pessimistic view of man as a "purely physiological creature"[103] with limitless "self-generating passions".[104] In this cynical view, "fear of death" is man's dominant passion.[105] Hobbes regarded the 'state of nature' as an undesirable situation from which man had to exit in order to achieve moral and social happiness.

---

[96]   *Id.*

[97]   *Id.* at 185.

[98]   *Id.*

[99]   *Id.* at 182.

[100]   *Id.* at 133.

[101]   *Id.* at 125.

[102]   *Id.* at 127.

[103]   *Id.* at 18.

[104]   *Id.* at 19.

[105]   *Id.* at 22.

Locke, in turn, presented an optimistic perspective of human nature. He famously stated that, "man is by nature morally good and that the evils in civil society are caused not by flaws in man's character, but by the bad effects of civil institutions".[106] In Locke's view, man enjoyed joy and peace in his 'state of nature'.[107] Thus, the incorrigible wrong concept of human nature that is present at the background of Locke's political theories is all too evident. In fact, Locke's view of human nature broadly reflects the Calvinist doctrine of the accursed and the elected and, consequently, ignores the shades of grey in every person. He says: "such men [referring to those who wrong others] are not under the ties of the common law of reason [and] have no other rule but that of force and violence, and so may be treated as beasts of prey".[108]

Locke's error resides in his conception of men being either good or evil. Notwithstanding, a superficial examination of reality, reason, science, and experience suffices to see that, as Edmund Burke states, man is more than just a "creature of emotions and the psychological". Indeed, man is "a complex organic compound of many biological, psychological, and spiritual elements, a dualism of flesh and spirit,"[109] in which not a single feature dominates the existential spectrum. As a result, "[p]olitics ought to be adjusted not to human reasonings, but to human nature, of which the reason is but a part, and by no means the greatest part".[110]

By boldly classifying men as good or evil, Locke departed from an erroneous –and superficial– perception of human nature that polluted the most important aspects of the political theory he built upon it.

Further increasing the degree of error in Locke's understanding of human nature is his random idea that "Adam created a perfect man".[111] No such idea could be entertained by the uninitiated in law, theology, or even social sciences. Had Adam been "perfect" we would live in another world, but unfortunately *res ipsa loquitur* [things speak by themselves].

Another point of Lockean self-contradiction relates to whether man is born a reasonable being. On one hand, Locke states that "[t]he law that was to govern Adam was the same that was to govern all his posterity, the

---

[106]   *Id.* at 145.

[107]   *Id.* at 131.

[108]   Locke, *supra note* 4, at 8.

[109]   Stanlis, *supra note* 296, at 186.

[110]   *Id.* at 168.

[111]   Locke, *supra note* 5, at 25.

law of reason". On the other hand, Adam's offspring, having entered the world by natural birth, produced them ignorant and *without the use of reason*.[112] Next, he concludes that, "we are born free, as *we are born rational*".[113]

Yet another contradiction lies in the fact at some instances he calls for the indissolubility of the marital bond[114] while at others he rejected such indissolubility.[115]

Both Hobbes and Locke proposed a common empirical theory of knowledge and mechanistic conception of human nature.[116] Locke specifically posited the "pursuit of pleasure" principle, according to which a "fundamentally egoistic human nature and behavior"[117] ruled in terms of pleasure and pain. Locke's "utilitarian strain co-joined with Hobbes' Epicurean ethics".[118]

While the rationalists showed aversion to "artificial institutions and government,"[119] the sentimentalists rejected Locke's optimist perception of human nature. Still, both rationalists and sentimentalists explained evil as originating in external social conditions that impeded the free expression of man's natural goodness.[120]

Jean Jacques Rousseau spearheaded the sentimentalist approach with his "man of sensibility"[121] theory. Similar to the Calvinist doctrine of the elected, Rousseau understood man as a creature "intrinsically morally sound [who] became corrupted by the external refinements and demands of his civil institutions".[122]

---

[112] *Id.*

[113] *Id.* at 27.

[114] *Id.* at 36 (stating that God "*made it necessary* that society of man and wife should be more lasting than of male and female amongst other creatures, that so their industry might be encouraged").

[115] *Id.* at 37 (finding that a man's "wife has in many cases a liberty to separate from him, where *natural right or their contract* allows it").

[116] *Id.* at 162 & 171 (Although "Locke's purely abstract or physiological conception of man," "was far more optimistic than the cynical and Epicurean philosophy of Hobbes, both assumed an egocentric pleasure-pain calculus").

[117] Stanlis, *supra note* 296, at 22.

[118] *Id.* at 22.

[119] *Id.* at 184.

[120] *Id.*

[121] *Id.* at 19 (citing Rousseau's 1762 *Contrat Social*).

[122] *Id.* at 127.

Thus, artificial institutions were usurpers of man's "natural rights" corrupting him and preventing him from living in civil society with the same freedom he had enjoyed in a 'state of nature.'[123]

In the Rousseaunian perspective, evils appeared "because men left simple 'nature' and lived under complex artificial institutions".[124] The abstract state of physical nature was supposed to be man's 'original' or 'natural' state. As a result, Rousseau proposed that a simple society, close to 'nature' "was morally superior to the complex and refined 'artificial' civil society of eighteenth-century Europe".[125] Anti-Christian rationalism and sentimentalism brought about a dramatic rupture from Western traditional natural law, yielding to a widespread Epicureanism. This rupture "wished to amend human nature by emancipating it from history".[126]

At the philosophical level, the "natural rights" philosophers preached a Manichean view of society in which artificial institutions and laws are "the sources of all the vices and moral miseries of mankind".[127] Per this unbounded faith in human nature, man is an innocent creature who has been perverted by artificial institutions.[128]

Response of Traditional Natural Law to the Rationalists' Erroneous Conception of Human Nature

Edmund Burke clearly identified the anti-Christian vein at the core of the 'natural rights' theory.[129] Rousseau's sensibility –he said– was "another form of Epicurean self-indulgence,"[130] and his emotionalism

supercharged eighteenth-century radical theory with a militant religious fervor. It enabled modern Epicureanism to disguise itself as a pseudo-religion, and to make claims as a full-fledged moral philosophy. It taught a personal religion of

---

[123] *Id.*

[124] *Id.* at 128.

[125] *Id.* at 127.

[126] *Id.* at 161.

[127] *Id.* at 152.

[128] *Id.*

[129] *Id.* at 192 (citing Burke's attack against Rousseau' sensibility in his 1791 *A Letter to a Member of the National Assembly*).

[130] *Id.*

social salvation through works alone, and that the dictates of right reason and the revelations of Christianity were no longer necessary.[131]

In contrast to Locke's *tabula rasa* theory, Burke replied that "man is not a blank sheet at birth; he is born with a mass of predispositions inherited from an incalculable past".[132] Man, by nature is a political animal, the heir of "an enormously complex historical tradition".[133] Burke went at lengths to express the perspective of traditional natural law concerning divine revelation and civil institutions:

> Historical continuity is a human form of divine revelation through political, legal, and literary documents; social monuments; the accumulated knowledge of the practical arts and sciences; moral philosophy; Christian Scripture; and Church doctrines and traditions. Through all this, history reveals the will of God in man's temporal affairs.[134]

In concordance with the traditional natural law doctrine, Burke expounds against the 'natural rights' theory that man is "a complex organic compound of many biological, psychological, and spiritual elements [and] a dualism of flesh and spirit".[135] He explains that there is no separation between reason and emotion in human nature; emotion too is a part of human nature, and is as capable of error and evil as logical reason.[136] Both emotion and reason act as "*corporate* guides to a true understanding of human nature".[137] For Burke, an exaltation of the passionate composition of man (whether evil or good passions govern him), demonstrated the affirmation of an inexistent conflict between nature and humanity.[138] He

---

[131] *Id.* at 193.

[132] *Id.* at 161.

[133] *Id.*

[134] *Id.* at 162.

[135] *Id.* at 186 (also stating that there is in man a "rich fusion of the senses, reason, and faith, of prejudices, passions, and intuitions, all enriched by fancy, imagination, and social habits").

[136] *Id.* at 168 (Burke stated, "leave a man to his passions, and you leave a wild beast to a savage and capricious nature").

[137] *Id.* at 169.

[138] *Id.* at 175 (Burke rejected the "oversimplified explanation of the causes of evil conditions in civil society, and [the] facile interpretation of history" [which] "ignored the illusions, passions, and vices common to all men… history consists, for the greater part, of the miseries brought upon the world by pride, ambition, avarice, revenge, lust, sedition, hypocrisy, ungoverned zeal, and all the train of disorderly appetites, which shake the public. These vices are the *causes* of those storms, and morals, laws, prerogatives, privileges, liberties, rights of men, are the *pretexts*").

went deep into the human heart when he recognized that this apparent conflict in which Epicureanism sought to exalt the private ego at the expense of the "natural law".[139] He added that the reputed conflict between nature and humanity:

> was the result of a false humility or excessive pride, and appeared because men could not achieve in practice the abstract perfection of their social and political theories".[140]

Burke rejected "the pleasure-pain calculus at the heart of the utilitarian strain in Locke's philosophy"[141] as an inherently false and rationalistic method, which corrupted man's moral sensibility, principles, and social nature. He also rejected the utilitarian pleasure-pain calculus in economics, "which was founded on avarice, in favor of a Christian conception of man and the universe".[142] Utilitarianism –Burke noted– "was indistinguishable from the ancient Epicurean principle that pleasure and enlightened self-interest were man's highest good".[143]

Quite contrary to Hobbes, Locke, and Rousseau, traditional natural law teaches that civil institutions are natural to man. In fact, nature is a corporate being and civil society is the result of organic development over a long period of time.[144] The radical and revolutionary idea of a "universal benevolence"[145] that would have existed in the 'state of nature' simply tended –in Burke's view– to destroy both the international and constitutional conceptions of the law of nations and "taught men to hate their country because they loved mankind".[146]

In sum, the 'natural rights' theory departed from a warped conception of human nature. The whole ideological edifice built upon it later by rationalism[147] and modernism was fraught with insuperable defects, and these

---

[139] *Id.* at 190.

[140] *Id.*

[141] *Id.* at 169.

[142] *Id.* at 174.

[143] *Id.* at 191.

[144] *Id.* at 164.

[145] *Id.* at 96.

[146] *Id.* at 101.

[147] *Id.* at 24 (In general, the speculative and rationalistic philosophers of the eighteenth century, such as "Hobbes, Spinoza, Locke, Pufendorf, Christian Wolff, Thomasius, Burlamaqui, Kant, Hegel, and even Bentham," treated the natural law as if it were geometry).

misconceptions are, in a fundamental way, contributors to the inhuman events that occurred in the Western world throughout the nineteenth and twentieth centuries.

J. *An Objective or Subjective 'Natural Rights' Theory?*

Leo Strauss rightly explains the distortion of traditional natural law wrought by the revolutionary theory of the 'state of nature.'[148] Traditional natural law is an objective "rule and measure,"[149] a binding order prior to and independent of the human will. The 'natural rights' theory is —in contrast— a series of 'rights' and subjective claims "originating in the human will".[150]

The first meaningful departure from the traditional conception of the natural law occurred with Thomas Hobbes, who in his novel proposition of an alleged 'state of nature,' inaugurated the modern secular approach to natural law. Key to his ideas had been William of Occam's denial of the existence of universals.[151] As natural law is universal, Occam's denial logically included natural law.

Another argument advanced by Hobbes was the destruction of the primacy of "law" or "reason" —considered now subjective or not universal concepts— and their substitution by "power" or "will". For Hobbes, self-preservation identified with self-interest and was an expression of his version of natural law. Building on Hobbes' ideas, Locke, in turn, held that his "greatest happiness"[152] principle required the possession of power as a necessary means. All of these 'rights' bunched together came to be identified later as "natural rights".

Therefore, the 'natural rights' theory is founded on an egocentric conception of human nature and upon the principle of power in which powers are called 'rights.'[153]

---

[148] *See*, Leo Strauss, *The Political Philosophy of Hobbes* (1936), and Natural Right and History (1953)).

[149] Stanlis, *supra note* 296, at XX.

[150] *Id.* at 137.

[151] *Id.* at 17.

[152] *Id.* at 290.

[153] *Id.* at 22.

K. *A Real or Hypothetical 'State of Nature'?*

With or without 'natural rights' theorists, the alleged existence of a purely imaginary 'state of nature' or a historical 'state of nature' has been long debated.[154]

Locke sustained the existence of a 'state of nature' as "an actual historical situation,"[155] as a "political society,"[156] or even as geographical[157] community,[158] not merely as a hypothetical assumption. The idea of 'primitivism' developed from Locke's proposition of a historical 'state of nature;'[159] that is, the belief "that society could best exist with practically no government at all".[160] The goal of abolishing the State and all "artificial institutions" due to their inherent "wickedness" was broadly embraced by the rationalistic political philosophers from the late seventeenth to the early nineteenth century.[161]

The British rationalists were particularly vociferous about the philosophical and political idea of a return to nature. For example, Mary Wollstonecraft held that nature is:

simple, clear, and uniform, and spontaneously apprehended by instinct or reason, whereas the 'artificial' customs and institutions of civil society are complex and obscure.[162]

Catherine Macaulay Graham, added that,

man was by nature morally sound[163] [and that therefore] the origin of evil is owed wholly by external forces and circumstances. Artificial institutions gave

---

[154] Rommen, *supra note* 10, at 97.

[155] Stanlis, *supra note* 296, at 138.

[156] *Id.* at 138.

[157] *Id.* at 94.

[158] *Id.* at 138.

[159] Thomas Paine in his *Rights* of *Man* also affirmed his belief in a historical 'state of nature').

[160] Stanlis, *supra note* 296, at 147.

[161] *Id.* at 149 (Mark Wilks, for instance, affirmed that "man's pride and depravity resulted from the increase in wealth and complexity of civil society, and that to fulfill all of man's economic needs, men had to live in civil society without governments, as in a simple state of nature"). *Id.*, at 151 (Sir Brooke Boothby's *A Letter to Edmund Burke* (1791) supported a "conscious antithesis between natural simplicity").

[162] Stanlis, *supra note* 296, at 141 (citing Mary Wollstonecraft, *A Vindication of the Rights of Man* (1790).

'the *opportunity* of committing crimes' and encouraged that 'very *depravity* of sentiment' from which crimes proceed".[164]

Joseph Priestley argued for a reversion to a state of nature, in which man "may enter into a new state of society, and adopt a new form of government"[165] for his overall betterment.

These philosophical ideas bred a political project which consisted in the abolition of the "European system of artificial institutions [for men] to enjoy the same liberty and 'rights' in civil society that they had known in the state of nature".[166]

The Response of Traditional Natural Law to the Historical 'State of Nature'

In 1793, Edmund Burke declared in the House of Commons that Locke's *Treatise on Civil Government* was the worst book ever written.[167] At the core of his criticism was his objection to the primitivism of the Lockean 'state of nature'.

Burke sustained that since man was an intrinsically political animal, the supposed 'state of nature' never existed. The reason was that "in a state of perfect nature there cannot exist any rights of any kind whatsoever".[168] That is, no man living alone can be said to have any rights. Rights only exist relationally to civil society. Therefore, the 'state of nature' is a "mere creature of the imagination".[169]

Arguendo, Burke asked that in the event that such a natural historical state never existed, what right did anyone have to control one another? And how could rulers produce evidence of having a God-given right to

---

[163] *Id.* at 143 (Catherine Macaulay Graham's *Observations on the Reflections of Burke* (1791)).

[164] *Id.*

[165] *Id.* at 147 (citing Joseph Priestley, Letters to Edmund Burke Occasioned by His Reflections (1791).

[166] *Id.* at 143.

[167] Stanlis, *supra note* 296, at 139 ("[i]n 1793 the Constitutional Society of Sheffield printed an abstract of Locke's Treatise on Civil Government, the preface of which stated: 'Edmund Burke, the Knight Errant of Feudality, declared in the House of Commons, that 'Locke's Treatise on Civil Government, was the worst book ever written'").

[168] *Id.* at 158.

[169] *Id.*

govern?[170] If such natural right to government did not exist, "then each man in civil society would be free to decide for himself whether or not he was bound by civil laws".[171] Ultimately, if man is not bound by civil laws he is free to voluntarily choose not to exit the 'state of nature' where he enjoyed all his freedom in his alleged 'state of nature.'[172] Obviously, since speculation would be conducive to utter social chaos and widespread unhappiness, this primitive or pre-civil 'natural rights' theory would be profoundly inhuman.

Hence –as traditional natural law teaches– it is God who willed that man live in society and the State is a necessary means[173] for man to live his temporal existence shaped by natural sin. Reality demonstrates that man "was born without his own consent into a historically developed civil society,[174] formed by the family, religious institutions, the government, race, nationality, communities. *Ergo*, 'artificial' or 'civil' institutions" are 'natural' to man.

Another essential criticism against Locke's political philosophy is the refusal of his theory of individual 'natural' freedom. In effect, man was never free not to abide by the natural rules that applied to him since the beginning. Quite the opposite, his freedom comes by "his willing adherence to the just rules and restrictions of his particular civil society,"[175] not from his adherence to a pact in order to exit the 'state of nature' as the rationalists had proposed.

L. *The 'Social Contract' as the Way Out from the 'State of Nature'*

Hobbes had proposed the notion of a 'social contract' through which men would have exited the 'state of nature.' That sort of irrevocable agreement[176] would have legitimated the legal sovereignty of the established authority. As the State brought order to a chaotic 'state of nature,'

---

[170] *Id.* at 137.

[171] *Id.* at 144.

[172] *Id.*

[173] *Id.* at 130.

[174] *Id.* at 131.

[175] *Id.* at 164.

[176] *Id.* at 207.

the "absolute will of the sovereign"[177] thus became the "only source of law"[178] and "imposed itself over right reason".[179]

For Locke, the way men exited from the nefarious 'state of nature' putting an end to it, was by the agreement they reached "together mutually to enter into one community, and make one body politic".[180] Access to this compact exclusively binds those men who "by their own consents ... make themselves members of some politic society".[181]

Based on his optimistic view of man, Locke is more revolutionary than Hobbes in that Locke "minimizes civic duties further by making the social contract revocable at will".[182] Locke's social contract is the only standard for determining the legitimacy and "continuation of government".[183] In effect, he argues that since man must have existed before governments did, "there necessarily was a time when governments did not exist".[184] He further adds that, consequently,

> [t]he individuals themselves, each in his own personal and sovereign right, entered into a compact with each other to produce a government. As a result, the social contract is the only mode in which governments have a right to arise, and the only principle on which they have a right to exist.[185]

Locke maintained that men entered into civil society to protect the "rights" they enjoyed in the 'state of nature.' Paramount among these rights was the protection of private property.[186] In other words, men renounce their property rights in favor of the community, which acquires the power to rule over them. Leo Strauss noted that "Locke's teaching on property, and his whole political philosophy, are revolutionary not only with regard to the Biblical tradition but with regard to the philosophic tra-

---

[177] *Id.* at 18.

[178] *Id.*

[179] *Id.*

[180] Locke, *supra note* 5, at 7.

[181] *Id.*

[182] Stanlis, *supra note* 296, at 23.

[183] *Id.* at 147.

[184] *Id.*

[185] *Id.*

[186] *Id.* at 138 (Locke argued that, "every man when he first incorporates himself into any commonwealth submits to the community those possessions which he has, or shall acquire").

dition".[187] In fact, his idea of the "revocable contract is even more revolutionary than his teaching on property".[188]

The Response of Traditional Natural Law to the Notion of the 'Social Contract'

A basic teaching of traditional natural law is that all men are born "in subjection to one great, immutable, pre-existing law,"[189] which is the Natural Law. As a result, implicit in man's connection with this immutable law is a conception of divine contract, in the sense that "God contracted with Himself never to be unjust to man".[190] And for this purpose, God gave man the natural law, whose postulates constitute what the rationalists called 'social contract.' As a result, the natural law is the moral standard in all human dealings. And for the very same reason, "man's relationship to civil society is a moral necessity; it cannot be voluntaristic"[191] as the 'social contract' notions propose. There is an inherent negation of truth and simple humanity behind the Lockean theory of a voluntary and revocable social contract, which in turn, is based upon a hypothetical, inexistent, 'state of nature.'[192] In definitive, society is indeed a contract, but not one that may be dissolved at pleasure.

Therefore, the very existence of the State is a natural consequence of man being a social being. For Edmund Burke, the State is the greatest and best gift of God to man.[193] The state of civil society was the absolutely necessary means by which man could live according to the natural law.[194] In consequence, the State may not be considered as nothing better than "a partnership agreement in things subservient"[195] only to a temporary and perishable nature and to be dissolved by the "fancy of the parties".[196] Quite the contrary, in his view, the State is "a partnership not only between those who are living, but also those who are dead, and those who

---

[187] *Id.*

[188] *Id.*

[189] *Id.* at 62.

[190] *Id.* at 71.

[191] *Id.* at 72.

[192] *Id.*

[193] *Id.* at 71.

[194] *Id.* at 128.

[195] *Id.* at 72.

[196] *Id.*

are to be born".[197] The State connects "the visible and invisible world, according to a fixed compact sanctioned by the inviolable oath".[198] The social contract was really "a fixed compact"[199] that

> God made with Himself and with man, sanctioned by an inviolable oath that the physical and moral universe God had created would not be changed by His or anyone's arbitrary will.[200]

This oath "did not mean that the state ... was unalterable, but that all changes [to the state had] to be made in conformity with the Natural Law".[201] In this context, "[t]he temporal state was a divine instrument, a necessary aid to grace".[202]

Historically, after the fall of the Western Roman Empire, feudalism arose in the low Middle Ages. In the feudal scheme, the vassal is given a spear "from the hand of some old and respected chief".[203] In this bond "[n]o man could stand out as an independent individual, but must have enlisted in one of these military fraternities ... [where he became] bound to his leader in the strictest dependence, which was confirmed by all oath, in a common vow for their mutual support in all dangers, and for the advancement of the honour of their common chief".[204] Burke explains that, "[t]his was the very first origin of civil, or rather military, government amongst the ancient people of Europe ... [and] arose from the connection ... between the person who gave the arms, or knighted the young man, and him that received them".[205] In addition, "amongst equals in condition, there could be no such bond, and this was supplied by confederacy. The first of these principles created the senior and the knight and the second produced the *conjurati fraters*".[206] Thus, in the European experience the case of feudalism is the closest example that could be found to Locke's alleged 'state of nature' philosophy.

---

[197] *Id.*

[198] *Id.*

[199] *Id.* at 207.

[200] *Id.* at 208.

[201] *Id.*

[202] *Id.*

[203] Edmund Burke, *An Abridgment of English History* (1757), *in* Rogers, *supra note* 18, at 541.

[204] *Id.*

[205] *Id.*

[206] *Id.*

M. *The French Revolution's Legal Codification of the "State of Nature"*

The Declaration of the Rights of Man adopted by the French National Assembly on August 26, 1789 was the historical culmination of the Lockean and Rousseauist "natural rights" theory. As a matter of fact, a core provision of the Declaration stated that, *"all men are by nature free, are equal in respect of rights, and continue so in society"*. Behind this statement is a terrifying revolutionary spirit that continues in every place and *époque*, recognizing nothing in society that obeys tradition or to the accumulated knowledge and experience of millennia and human wisdom. Take for instance, what a leading member of the French National Assembly declared prior to the adoption of the Declaration:

> All institutions in France crown the misfortune of the people: to make the people happy all must be renewed; change its ideas; change its laws; changes its morals; change men; change things; change the words; yes, to destroy everything; because everything must be created anew.[207]

The ongoing revolutionary spirit immersed in the 'natural rights' theory, of which the 'state of nature' idea is an essential part of, calls for a permanent rebellion of man against all things that are natural to him: established institutions, traditions, customs, accumulated wisdom, and talent.[208] In fact, the French Revolution codified core ideas of the 'natural rights' theory under the assumption that "civilization as it actually existed was a kind of hell [and that] man could be redeemed socially only by destroying civilization"[209] returning to the state of nature, that is, to a "theoretically perfect primitive or simple civilization".[210] For this speculative hope to occur, a systematic political movement of destruction was necessary.

The idea of a society of entitlement stemmed from the 'natural rights' theory, that is, of a society "of rights without duties,"[211] Ultimately, as Edmund Burke predicted, a civil society based on hypothetical 'rights' arising from "an original 'state of nature' would end by destroying men's real civil rights".[212]

---

[207]   Stanlis, *supra note* 8, at 134 (citing M. Rabaud de St. Etienne).

[208]   *Id.* at 130 (citing Edmund Burke who had stated that, "as man's nature was essentially civil, his 'rights' as a citizen were determined by the conventions of his society").

[209]   *Id.* at 134.

[210]   *Id.*

[211]   *Id.* at XXXII.

[212]   *Id.* at 130.

N. *The Empty "Principle of Equality"*
Advanced by the 'Natural Rights' Theory

The teachings of the fathers of traditional natural law always understood "equality" firstly within the theological context. In this vein, the notion of equality is, above all, metaphysical, and consists in the contemplation of a God who, in his mysterious mercy, created man and woman as a species, to partake of His creation, without any differences in origin, dignity, or destiny.

It was Locke who famously pontificated about a 'state of nature' considered as a 'state of equality.'[213] However, Locke –the master of wordiness and confusion that he was– did not convey a clear conceptual idea of 'equality.' In fact, on one hand, he understood equality as meaning that "every man may have the same rights that are granted to others".[214] However, he also propounded a somehow cryptic notion stating that when men "enter into society [they] give up the equality, liberty, and executive power they had in the state of nature into the hands of the society".[215] As a result, if man was originally 'equal' and then through the social contract relinquished his 'equality' into the State, then how could Locke explain that man was likewise 'equal' before and after the social contract?

Despite its undefined concept, the idea of equality found a secure port during the War of American Independence. Few philosophical/constitutional ideas are more cherished by the American public than the notion of 'equality.' The U.S. Declaration of Independence states that, "all men are created equal". However, the meaning of equality, its scope and application remain an issue as contentious as it has always been since the inception of the American democratic experiment. The American conception of "equality" was composed of very specific elements, and entailed a reaction against the old European traits. The most important elements of the *original* American concept of equality are:

(a) *The Dissolution of a Concentrated Land Ownership System*: The European land organization from which the colonizers ran away was the basis of the very territorial aristocracy,[216] which they sought to overcome. At the center of the new political project, Americans created a system in

---

[213] Locke, *supra note* 5, at 2 ("[T]his equality of men by nature [is] evident in itself.)".

[214] Locke, *supra note* 41, at 148.

[215] Locke, *supra note* 5, at 59.

[216] *Id.* at 25.

which all limitations concerning the quality, amount, and transferability of land were eliminated. The new laws greatly favored the division of property[217] in a scheme where the holder of the land was also the proprietor of the land.[218] Thus, tenancy of the land on a first-come-first served basis, protected by favorable laws,[219] and a wave of colonizers escaping scarcity created the perfect environment for a love of equality understood as the guarantee of even access to land ownership.

(b) *System of Inheritance*: the ancient European societal system rested upon the landed aristocracies that arose after the fall of the Western Roman Empire. The Judeo-Christian primogeniture structure was key to the class system under which "the eldest son, inherit[ed] the greater part of the property and almost all [of] the rights of the family, becomes the chief and to a certain extent the master of his brothers".[220]

Obviously, one of the first political/economical decisions of the American settlers was to abolish primogeniture, and to remove inheritance differences based on gender. The underlying idea was to facilitate the circulation of wealth outside of the nuclear family in a faster and more evenly distribute manner.[221] As a consequence, the abolition of the primogeniture scheme brought an unstoppable energy to the second sons of the family in the nascent American Republic.

As Tocqueville explains, in the American experiment, "the law of inheritance was the last step to equality,"[222] because the abolition of primogeniture had "reduced all to one level,"[223] in what he called "the permanent equality of property".[224]

(c) *Political Power of the Clergy*: In tune with its Puritan roots, the American Republic replaced the millenary clergy scheme for one in which every citizen is an actual or potential clergy member at any given time. Equality, in this regard, was understood as the discontinuance of the

---

[217] *Id.* at 175.

[218] *Id.* at 25.

[219] *Id.* at 39 (In America the "equal partition of property is established by law").

[220] *Id.* at 481.

[221] *Id.* at 41 ("[W]hen the idea of family becomes vague, indeterminate, and uncertain, a man thinks of his present convenience.").

[222] *Id.* at 39.

[223] *Id.* at 42.

[224] *Id.*

levitical restriction to a clergy class or the notion of the Christian notion of an institutional clergy.

(d) *Commercial Monopolies*: The old European monopolistic systems based on rank and nobility yielded to a format characterized by an improved development in the "commerce of manufactures [that] created so many new elements of equality among men".[225]

(e) *Religious Equality*: In tune with the Protestant cultural ethos shaping American society since the mid-seventeenth century, the new Republic strongly proclaimed the Christian notion that "all men are equal in the sight of God".[226] This metaphysical approach[227] translated into a notion of equality according to which no religious animosity would be tolerated "because all religion is respected and no sect is predominant".[228]

(f) *Social Equality*:[229] widespread economic betterment in the new American Republic triggered a "progressive development of social equality,"[230] which Americans early on called "equality of condition".[231]

(g) *Political Equality*: A logical result deriving from the broad dissemination of wealth is the conviction that property is accessible to everyone.[232] Therefore, economic equality begets political equality.[233] It is precisely in the evolution of the concept of "political equality" where the hidden dangers posited by the original American democratic experiments first started to show its philosophical cracks.[234]

With this as background, it is easier to perceive how since the early twentieth century, Western societies have steadily –and dangerously–

---

[225] *Id.* at 5.

[226] *Id.* at 14.

[227] *Id.* at 6 ("Protestantism proclaimed that all men are equally able to find the road to heaven").

[228] *Id.* at 90.

[229] *Id.* at 191 ("Anglo-Americans settled in the New World in a state of social equality").

[230] *Id.* at 8.

[231] *Id.* at 16.

[232] *Id.* at 137.

[233] *Id.* at 143 ("the democratic institutions of the United States, joined to the physical constitution of the country, are the cause ... of the prodigious commercial activity of the inhabitants").

[234] *Id.* at 45 ("there exists also in the human heart a depraved taste for equality, which impels the weak to attempt to lower the powerful to their own level and reduces men to prefer equality in slavery to inequality with freedom.").

moved from the notion of equality of opportunity, to an idea of egalitarianism according to which even the "allocation of talents and abilities must be regarded as 'arbitrary'".[235] These leveling tendencies ignore human nature, "political and economic realities, as well as recorded history".[236] The whole equality movement has evolved "from a guarantee of equality of opportunity to equality of results".[237] The equalitarian trend has been achieved by coercion, and coercion necessarily implies the violation of the rights of others.[238] In contrast, experience and reason show that "[liberty is by its nature inegalitarian, because living creatures differ in intelligence, ambition, courage, perseverance and all else that makes for success".[239]

Locke's ideas lay, again, at the origin of the egalitarian philosophy. He postulated that the 'state of nature' was a "state of perfect equality" where "no superiority or jurisdiction of one over another"[240] existed. Yet he never explained his notion of "perfect equality" or even that of equality itself,[241] leaving many crucial questions opened for future elaboration.

In his proposals on equality, Locke once again mixed rights with wrongs. For instance, contrary to his idea of a "natural state of equality" he mentions several natural grounds of inequality amongst men: *e.g.*, age, virtue, merit, birth, and gratitude.[242] He strives to save the day by explaining that equality means "that equal right that every man hath to his natural freedom, without being subjected to the will or authority of any other man".[243]

So imprecise is his concept of 'equality' that the latter definition could explain equality as physical liberty, *i.e.*, an absence of slavery, that is, as a negative concept. For if he was referring to "political" freedom, his proposal was wrong because most men who live in society have never been asked whether they consented in the existing social order in which they

---

[235] Dougherty, supra note 7, at 11.

[236] *Id.* at 12.

[237] *Id.*

[238] *Id.*

[239] Richard Pipes, *Property and Freedom* (New York: Alfred A. Knopf, 1999), at 283 (*cited* in Dougherty, *supra note* 7, at 13.

[240] Locke, *supra note* 5, at 4.

[241] *Id.* at 24 (famously saying "I cannot be supposed to understand all sorts of equality").

[242] *Id.*

[243] *Id.*

happen to find themselves or, *a fortiori*, if they ever wanted to live in society whatsoever. Therefore, Locke's understanding of equality as a situation that implies the freedom of not "being subjected to the will or authority of any other man" may not logically refer to political life. The definition logically refers to contractual freedom. And in this matter, traditional natural law takes no issue with Locke, since he merely repeated what St. Thomas of Aquinas had masterfully explained before: that mutually agreed contracts must be respected.

Traditional Natural Law's Rejection of the Abstract Idea of Equality

Against Locke's ideas on equality, Blackstone had also spoken:

The principles of Mr. Locke would have levelled all distinctions of honour, rank, offices, and property; would have annihilated the sovereign power, and in consequence repealed all positive laws...[244]

Likewise, Edmund Burke, with traditional natural law ideas in the background, recalled that Thomas Paine[245] had attempted "to destroy as 'unnatural' all inherited or acquired social distinctions".[246] Burke also suggested that "particular attention should be given to the abstract and oftentimes empty concept of *equality* at any price".[247] He simply observed certain facts of nature, such as that nature is unequal, some live and others die, some are naturally stronger than others, some work harder than others, and some prosper in a naught while others strive their whole lives for the *minimum*.[248] He too observed that in civil life there is much diversity amongst men, according to their birth, education, professions, period of their lives, residence in towns or in the country, and several ways of acquiring and fixing property. He believed that God created "many natural differences among mankind,"[249] according to infinite circumstances that set men apart. He distinguished the natural inequality of man in *aptitudes* from the natural equality of man in *dignitas*. Equality in *dignity* really means equal opportunity for everyone to prosper, and no discrimination in

---

[244] Blackstone, Commentaries, I, 213, *cited* in Stanlis, *supra note* 296, at 136.

[245] Burke, *Letters on the Affairs of Ireland, supra note* 196, at 463 (calling Paine, "[t]his protestant apostle").

[246] Stanlis, *supra note* 8, at 191.

[247] *Id.*

[248] *Id.*

[249] *Id.* at 111.

the sense that every effort should be met with equal reward regardless of ancillary or accidental attributes. Hence, the traditional natural law "conception of equality centered in equity ... as members of the same species, and also in an equal regard for their individual differences".[250]

In that sense, the 'natural rights' idea that everybody enjoys an inherent right to everything and anything was –for Burke– particularly "dangerous and fallacious".[251] The hypothetical theory of equal "rights of man" in a 'state of nature' could not be established, except by ignoring and leveling out "all the natural and inherited, preferences, and local loyalties found in civil society under natural and constitutional law".[252] In sum, Burke advocated for a "natural aristocracy' of talents and virtues in every free, well-ordered and just society".[253]

O. *The 'Natural Rights' Theory on Majoritarianism*

Next to equality, Locke's thoughts on "majoritarianism" compose the backbone of the 'natural rights' theory. In his famous *Two Treatises of Government*, Locke proposed that popular sovereignty centered in the legislative power of the absolute and arbitrary will of Parliament alone, as based upon popular support.[254] Despite his recognition that at some point: "by nature government was monarchical,"[255] he rejected monarchical absolutism favoring the majority rule.[256] Next in his political philosophical spiral was the concept of an absolutist majoritarianism:

> out of a state of nature unite into a community must be understood *to give up all the power* necessary to the ends for which they unite into society, to the majority of the community.[257]

Locke's absolutist majoritarianism went even further to sacralize the legislative branch of government as the "supreme authority".[258] In these

---

[250] *Id.* at 191.

[251] *Id.* at 103.

[252] *Id.* at 94.

[253] *Id.* at 191.

[254] *Id.* at 12.

[255] Locke, *supra note* 5, at 48.

[256] *Id.* at 44 ("[E]very one is bound by that consent to be concluded by the majority").

[257] *Id.* at 45.

[258] *Id.* at 62.

terms, "the legislative is not only the supreme power of the common-wealth, but sacred and unalterable".[259] Apocalyptically, he retorts that, "when the legislative is broken or dissolved, dissolution and death fol-low".[260] However –and consistent with Locke's overall inconsistencies– on the one hand, he recognized that the limited nature of the legislative power "can never have a right to destroy, enslave, or designedly to im-poverish the subjects".[261] He reinforced the idea of a limited legislative power by recognizing that there remains in people a sort of residual "su-preme power to remove or alter the legislative".[262] In synthesis, he states that, "the community may be said in this respect to be always the supreme power".[263] On the other hand, nevertheless, he confuses his audience fur-ther when he asserts the primacy of the executive branch ("[w]here the legislative and executive power are in distinct hands ... the good of the society requires that several things should be left to the discretion of him that has the executive power".[264]

Ultimately, one is never on a sure footage with Locke, not even in the most basic things. He remains a master of wordiness and confusion.

The Response of Traditional Natural Law Toward the Majoritarianism Principle

The response from traditional natural law to the enlightened idea of majoritarianism –per which all moral rights and moral wrongs are deter-mined by the collectivity– may well be summarized in these two opposite equations: Locke's *"Salus populi suprema lex"* [the health of the people is the supreme law],[265] and *"Voluntas Dei suprema lex"* [God's will is the supreme law].

In this respect, Edmund Burke asserted, "I am not one of those who think that the people are never in the wrong"[266] for to exercise authority

---

[259] *Id.* at 61, 68.

[260] *Id.* at 97.

[261] *Id.* at 62.

[262] *Id.* at 68.

[263] *Id.* at 69.

[264] *Id.* at 74.

[265] *Id.* at 73.

[266] Edmund Burke, Thought on the Present Discontents (1770), in Rogers, supra note 18, at 125.

"and to controul together is contradictory and impossible".[267] He criticized altogether the revolutionary idea of a *majority* "as if it were a law of our original nature [and considered it] one of the most violent fictions of positive law".[268] He further added:

> …the claim of the minority to protection by the law against the will of the majority functioning as the positive law dearly shows that there exists prior to the positive law an a priori element of a material character which qualifies the legislative will as just or unjust.[269]

Burke remarked the true essence of the 'natural rights' idea of equality with a bright corollary:

> …equal want, equal wretchedness, equal beggary, and on the part of the petitioners, a woeful, helpless and desperate disappointment. Such is the event of all compulsory equalizations. They pull down what is above. They never raise what is below.[270]

P. *On the Twisted Concept of Toleration*

Locke's *Letter on Toleration* became the early catechism of the seventeenth century rationalist philosophers. Passionately, Edmund Burke unleashed his views on the "large and liberal [concept of toleration],"[271] about which he said, "is in reality a cruel and insidious religious persecution,"[272] a new persecution "not against a variety in conscience, but against all conscience [which] treats all religion with scorn [and] united the opposite evils of intolerance and of indifference".[273]

---

[267] Burke, An Appeal from the New to the Old Whigs in Consequence of Some Late Discussions in Parliament, Relative to the Reflections on the French Revolution, *supra* note 190, at 522.

[268] *Id.* at 524 ("the laws in many countries to *condemn* require more than a mere majority; less than an equal number to acquit. In our judicial trials, we require unanimity to condemn or to absolve. In some incorporations one man speaks for the whole; in others, a few.").

[269] Rommen, *supra note* 10, at 141.

[270] Edmund Burke, *Thoughts and Details on Scarcity* (1795), *in* Rogers, *supra note* 18, at 250.

[271] Burke, An *Appeal from the New to the Old Whigs in Consequence of Some Late Discussions in Parliament, Relative to the Reflections on the French Revolution, su-pra* note 190, at 495.

[272] *Id.*

[273] *Id.*

In definitive, the pretended "toleration" of the 'natural rights' theory is nothing but the persecution of the traditional natural law doctrine.

Q. *How the 'Natural Rights' Theory Planted the Seeds for the Destruction of Matrimony and of the Family*

Traditional natural law has been unwavering in recognizing that the right to marriage is a fundamental human right,[274] and not a "cultural product" malleable at will.[275] Its foundation lies in the biological difference between the genders that naturally allow for the perpetuation of the species, and is a perpetual testimony to the fundamental difference in dignity between man and animal. In consequence, what is natural is true, and what is true is good. Early on, Canon Law recognized the natural law character of the right to marriage,[276] and added external formalities for the validity of marriage, which were aimed at mainly protecting women from "deception, dishonor, and abandonment".[277]

The Encyclical letter Rerum Novarum of 1891 called the right to marriage, a "natural law which may not be limited by human laws".[278] The 1983 Pope John Paul II's Apostolic Exhortation letter *Familiaris Consortio* expressly said that, "the Church openly and strongly defends the rights of the family against the intolerable usurpations of society and the State".[279] In sum, canon law and traditional natural law consecrate, recognize, protect, and defend the right to marriage between a man and a woman as "a fundamental right of the human person".[280]

---

[274] Paolo Scoponi, I Divieti Matrimoniali in Casi Singoli (Editrice Pontificia Università Gregoriana, Roma 2011), at 7 (referring to the "natural right to marriage.").

[275] *Id.* at 11.3.

[276] *Id.* at 17 (stating that Gratian's Decretum (1140) expressly recognized the "centrality of the *ius connubii* [right to marriage] in the matrimonial system of the Church.").

[277] *Id.* at 23.

[278] Pope Leo XIII's Encyclical Letter Rerum Novarum, May 15, 1891, n. 645.

[279] Pope John Paul II's Apostolic Exhortation letter Familiaris Consortio, November 22, 1981, n. 46.

[280] Scoponi, *supra* note 563, at 38.

CHAPTER VI:

THE INROADS OF THE 'NATURAL RIGHTS' THEORY INTO THE FOUNDING DOCUMENTS OF THE UNITED STATES OF AMERICA

1. *The Puritanical Political-Religious Principles and their Relationship to Traditional Natural Law*

Puritanism "was almost as much a political theory as a religious doctrine".[1] The English Pilgrims were Puritan.[2] In this context, the influential Puritan lawyer John Winthrop gave a powerful speech in 1630 on the basic principles upon which the political and religious life of the new American colonies would be based.[3] Winthrop laid five principles: (1) the colonies would be a model of Christian society[4] and there would be no poor within it; (2) the colonists would achieve self-government in both church and politics; (3) the colonists would see that everybody was educated; (4) the colonies would be a "city on a hill," that is, a covenantal people created by God; and (5) those who jeopardize the community would be severely punished by the community, on God's behalf.[5]

Thus its possible to perceive the intimate connection between the 'natural rights' theory and these Puritanical political/philosophical ideas.

---

[1] De Tocqueville, supra *note* 504, at 28-9.

[2] *Id.* at 28 ("the Pilgrims, belonged to that English sect the austerity of whose principles had acquired for them the name of Puritans.").

[3] John Winthrop, Winthrop Papers, 1:302-3 (*cited* in Matthew S. Holland, Thomas Jefferson. Religious Beliefs and Political Doctrines *in Lectures on Religion and the Founding of the American Republic* (John W. Welch & S. Fleming, eds., Brigham Young University Press, Provo, Utah, 2003), at 86.

[4] De Tocqueville, supra *note* 504, at 32-3 ("the customs of the community were even more austere and puritanical than the laws").

[5] Holland, supra *note* 572, at 86.

2. *The Strengths De Tocqueville Saw in the American Democratic Experiment*

De Tocqueville identified several elements that, in his view, demonstrated the strength of the American democratic experiment, namely:

A. *The Democratic Ideal of Self-Government*

De Tocqueville called this principle, "the doctrine of the sovereignty of the people".[6] This rule of government pivoted around a few, but profound ideals: the appointment by the colonies of their own magistrates, the power to conclude peace or declare war, to pass their own laws police regulations, enact their own laws,[7] to allow the free intervention of the people in public matters, to decide their own taxation, to make their representatives accountable, to enjoy and protect their own personal liberty, and to conduct their trials by jury.[8]

De Tocqueville found that even before the colonies' independence, the republic was already established in every township"[9] at the colonies. Political life revolved around the local level[10] in a way that "was so perfectly natural [that] seems to come directly from the hand of God,"[11] that is, according to traditional natural law. Free local institutions constituted the very foundation of the political structure of the new republic.[12]

Next to the principle of self-determination present in the political life of the colonies –whose central idea was that "the office might be powerful and the officer insignificant"[13]– was the principle of separation of powers. The structure of power in the colonies was divided among "innumerable functionaries and officers". [14]

In addition, prior to their independence, the American colonies had lived under the traditional natural law principle of subsidiarity, which had

---

6   De Tocqueville, *supra note* 504, at 24.

7   *Id.* at 31.

8   *Id.* at 33.

9   *Id.* at 34.

10   *Id.* at 51.

11   *Id.* at 48.

12   *Id.* at 49 ("municipal institutions constitute the strength of free nations.").

13   *Id.* at 56.

14   *Id.* at 54.

shown them that "the collective strength of the citizens will always conduce more efficaciously to the public welfare than the authority of the government,"[15] and that, the "sum of . . . private undertakings far exceeds all that the government could have done".[16] The historical background of this social and economic structure based on subsidiarity had come from the existence of a strong middle class in England, where "the stronghold of Puritanism continued"[17] to rest.

Besides these principles, as De Tocqueville perceived that the colonies had a strong respect for the law.[18]

In summary, all these democratic principles which emanated from the teachings of traditional natural law, found the American colonies at the time of their independence with a favorable predisposition toward democracy, which in turn spearheaded economic growth, the diffusion of "wealth and comfort, promote(d) public spirit, and fortifie(d) the respect for law in all classes of society".[19]

B. *A Purer Morality at the Personal and Collective Levels*

De Tocqueville noticed that the democratic mindset of the American colonies was conducive to an increase in the morals of the people.[20] Morality and religion were inextricably united amongst the early Americans; moreover, religion was considered "as the safeguard of morality, and morality as the best security of law and the surest pledge of the duration of freedom".[21]

Thus, the public morality of the people qualified as "one of the great general causes to which the maintenance of a democratic republic in the United States is attributable".[22]

---

[15] *Id.* at 64.

[16] *Id.* at 68.

[17] *Id.* at 29.

[18] *Id.* at 68 (stating that "[i]n America [...] no one renders obedience to man, but to justice and to law").

[19] *Id.* at 126.

[20] *Id.* at 25.

[21] *Id.* at 37.

[22] *Id.* at 179.

C. *The American Experiment as the Fruit of a Religious Enterprise*

The Mayflower Compact begins with an unequivocal invocation: "[I]n the Name of God".[23] It later states that its goal is the "advancement of the Christian faith".[24] Besides the innumerable sects existing in the colonies, they all "preach(ed) the same moral law,"[25] "Christian morality".[26]

De Tocqueville was adamantly recognized that the Christian religion "directs the customs of the community, and, by regulating domestic life, it regulates the state".[27] Coupled with piety, there was a strong attachment to "democratic and republican institutions"[28] from the part of the Christian sects. In this scheme of things, De Tocqueville saw that Americans held religion "to be indispensable to the maintenance of republican institutions [and this opinion] belongs to the whole nation and to every rank of society".[29]

De Tocqueville saw that despite being a great minority in numbers Catholicism had pivotal strength in the nascent American democratic experiment. He alluded to Catholics as "the most republican and the most democratic class in the United States".[30] Key within its push for democracy was that Catholicism was "one of the most favorable to equality of condition among men,"[31] unlike Protestantism "which generally tends to make men independent more than to render them equal".[32]

D. *Entrepreneurship*

Much has been said about the American entrepreneurial spirit, but to that effect a striking quote from De Tocqueville suffices:

---

[23]   *Id.* at 29.

[24]   *Id.*

[25]   *Id.* at 182.

[26]   *Id.*

[27]   *Id.* at 183.

[28]   *Id.* at 182.

[29]   *Id.* at 185.

[30]   *Id.* at 180.

[31]   *Id.*

[32]   *Id.* at 181.

In America it sometimes happens that the same person tills his field, builds his dwelling, fashions his tools, makes his shoes, and weaves the coarse stuff of which his clothes are composed. This is prejudicial to the excellence of the work but it powerfully contributes to awaken the intelligence of the workman.[33]

E. *Extensive Public Education*

The education of the people was one of the key tenets of the Mayflower Puritans.[34] Mandatory education for children was imposed and strictly enforced in every American town.[35] A strong connection between the instruction of the people and the support for the democratic scheme existed from the inception of the American colonies.[36]

F. *A Politically Decentralized Government System*

The American constitutional system was conceived as an amalgam of decentralized units, called the states, which has nothing of "either centralized or hierarchical in its constitution".[37]

G. *A Strong Independent Judiciary*

In comparative terms, the American judiciary is perhaps the strongest branch of government around the world. Their power to overrule the legislature is directly connected to the survival of democracy.[38] American democracy makes no pretense that judges are not political functionaries in the republican model of government.[39]

Notwithstanding its own power,[40] the American judiciary has self-imposed several limitations concerning its role. Judges must issue their

---

[33] *Id.* at 280.

[34] Holland, *supra note* 572, at 86.

[35] De Tocqueville, supra *note* 504, at 35.

[36] *Id.* at 190.

[37] *Id.* at 56; *id.*, at 61 ("in the United States there is no centralized administration and no hierarchy of public functionaries").

[38] *Id.* at 77 (stating that it is "one of the most powerful barriers ... against the tyranny of political assemblies").

[39] *Id.* at 72.

[40] *Id.* at 75 ("few laws can escape the searching analysis of the judicial power").

decisions "based on the *Constitution* rather than on the *laws*,"[41] and they act only when called upon.[42]

H. *The Federal Constitution*

In a sense, the Federal Constitution represents a continuity of the "republican form of government"[43] established in it, with the colonial system. It was at the local level –in "townships and the provincial assemblies"[44]– where the taste for a republican government was first established in North America.

I. *A Limited Central Government*

Coupled with the strong power of the local governments, the Founders designed a Central Government that was meant to take care of those areas where the local levels –for different reasons– were unable to be efficient.[45] De Tocqueville was adamant to state that the federal system is "one of the combinations most favorable to the prosperity and freedom of man".[46]

J. *Freedom of the Press*

De Tocqueville detected that the underlying idea behind the freedom of the press in America was that, "to enjoy the inestimable benefits that [it] ensures, it is necessary to submit to the inevitable evils that it creates".[47] He went onto call the freedom of the press as "the chief democratic instrument of freedom"[48] that is intrinsically connected with the sovereignty

---

[41]   *Id.* at 74.

[42]   *Id.* at 73; *id.* at 74 (stating that judges "cannot act until they cause has been duly brought before the court").

[43]   *Id.* at 83.

[44]   *Id.*

[45]   *Id.* at 84 ("the sovereignty of the Union is limited and incomplete").

[46]   *Id.*

[47]   *Id.* at 96.

[48]   *Id.* at 592.

of the people.[49] In fact, he perceived that the freedom of the press was "the only cure for the evils that equality may produce".[50]

However, De Tocqueville also saw the dangers that the freedom of the press was exposed to; as well as, the errors to which that an undeterred freedom of the press could lead to. He perceived that when the press becomes uniform in its views and "adopt(s) the same line of conduct, their influence in the long run becomes irresistible [in the] public opinion".[51] He warned that the hammering of a particular perspective by a uniform press, particularly in times of philosophical and political confusion,[52] would cause many social dangers in America.[53] He perceived this danger increased by what he saw was the lower intellectual capabilities of those involved in the American press.[54]

K. *The Right of Association*

The right of association is "almost as inalienable in its nature as the right of personal liberty,"[55] and acts as a "necessary guarantee against the tyranny of the majority".[56] Perhaps in few nations is this right so entrenched with the "manners and customs of the people"[57] as it is in America. As it has been the case since the ancient Roman Empire, associations in America are established for the people "to promote public safety, commerce, industry, morality and religion".[58]

---

[49] *Id.* at 94.

[50] *Id.* at 591.

[51] *Id.* at 99.

[52] *Id.* at 96-7 ("[I]n America three quarters of the enormous sheet [of a journal] are filled with advertisements").

[53] *Id.* at 99 (stating that "[w]hen once the Americans have taken up an idea . . . nothing is more difficult than to eradicate it from their minds.").

[54] *Id.* at 97 (saying that since the press is free in America, competition is greater, and "as the competition prevents any considerable profit, persons of much capacity are rarely led to engage in these undertakings."); *id.* at 97 ("[t]he journalists of the United States are generally in a very humble position, with a scanty education and a vulgar turn of mind").

[55] *Id.* at 104.

[56] *Id.* at 103.

[57] *Id.*

[58] *Id.* at 100.

3. *The Weaknesses De Tocqueville Saw in the American Democratic Experiment*

De Tocqueville embarked in a full review of disturbing aspects of the American democratic experiment that –due to their stark opposition to traditional natural law– threatened its own existence.

A. *Slavery*

In no other aspect of American social and political life was the deviation from traditional natural law more evident than concerning the value of human dignity.[59] In fact, the American republic embraced slavery since its very beginning.[60]

a. *With respect to the Indians*

De Tocqueville took notice of the many evils that befell onto them at the hands of the British:

a) *Expulsion from their Lands*: Before colonization, the Indians "were the sole inhabitants of the wilds [and] their wants were few".[61] After having dispersed the Indians and "driven them into the deserts [the British] condemned them to a wandering life, full of inexpressible sufferings".[62]

In a sense, there was the inevitability of the disaster that the contact[63] between the Europeans and the Indians would ensue.[64] It is also true that so much disregard to the dignity of the Indians was utterly unnecessary[65] and could only be explained –never justified– by several of the philosoph-

---

[59] *Id.* at 201 (observing that in America "the European is to the other races of mankind what man himself is to the lower animals: he makes them subservient to his use, and when he cannot subdue he destroys them").

[60] *Id.* at at 26-7 ("slavery … dishonors labor; it introduces idleness into society, and with idleness, ignorance and pride, luxury and distress").

[61] *Id.* at 205.

[62] *Id.* at 202.

[63] *Id.* at 215 ("nations as well as men require time to learn, whatever may be their intelligence and their zeal").

[64] *Id.* at 219-220 ("it is the misfortune of Indians to be brought into contact with a civilized people").

[65] *Id.* at 208 ("[T]he expulsion of the Indians often takes place at the present day in a regular and, as it were, a legal manner").

ical and religious foundations of the north American settlers, which had irremediably deviated from traditional natural law concerning human nature.

De Tocqueville added a grim corollary to the fate of the Indians at the mercy of the British:

> if they continue barbarous, they are forced to retire; if they attempt to civilize themselves, the contact of a more civilized community subjects them to oppression and destitution.[66]

b) *Continuous Wretchedness*: Hunger, war, and misery never abandoned the Indians since the arrival of the British to the North American lands.[67] The colonizing policies implemented by the British made the disarray in which the Indians lived before the colonization even more chaotic.[68]

Existence of the Indians as a nation became impossible.[69] The inevitability of their demise[70] was further demonstrated in De Tocqueville's perception in that, "when the side on which the physical force lies also possesses an intellectual superiority, the conquered party seldom becomes civilized; it retreats or is destroyed".[71]

The Federal government was not only unable to stop the debacle, but moreover its own policies greatly contributed to its development.[72]

Drawing a parallel between the treatment of the Indians by the Spanish, De Tocqueville observed that:

> The Spaniards were unable to exterminate the Indian race ... nor did they succeed even in wholly depriving it of its rights; but the Americans of the United States have accomplished this twofold purpose with singular felicity, tranquilly, legally, philanthropically, without shedding blood, and without violating a sin-

---

[66]   *Id.* at 216.

[67]   *Id.* at 207 ("[H]unger is in the rear, war awaits them, and misery besets them on all sides.").

[68]   *Id.* at 202 ("[T]he moral and physical condition of these tribes continually grew worse, and they became more barbarous").

[69]   *Id.* at 207 ("living in the immensity of the desert like an outcast in civilized society [...] their nation has ceased to exist.").

[70]   *Id.* at 209 (it is "irremediable [...] I believe that the Indian nations of North America are doomed to perish").

[71]   *Id.* at 213.

[72]   *Id.* at 216 (alluding that the Federal government "has undertaken to transport [the Indians] into remote regions at the public cost.").

gle great principle of morality in the eyes of the world. It is impossible to destroy men with more respect for the laws of humanity.[73]

b. *With respect to the Black Race*

De Tocqueville noticed the skewed natural law connotation of the reasoning used by the British to enslave the black race,[74] stating that when they:

> chose their slaves from a race differing from their own ... They first violated every right of humanity by their treatment of the Negro, and they afterwards informed him that those rights were precious and inviolable.[75]

The British brought slavery back in utter violation of traditional natural law.[76] Hence, the iniquity of the 'natural rights' theory that taught that all men were equal, and at the same time enslaved half of its population.[77]

De Tocqueville prophesized with respect to the troubles that would threaten the future of the American republic *as a consequence* of the slavery that she had promoted.[78] He crowned his prophesies based on racial slavery by saying that, "[i]f ever America undergoes great revolutions, they will be brought about by the presence of the black race on the soil of the United States".[79]

He foresaw that complete harmony between the races would be close to impossible,

> Hitherto wherever the whites have been the most powerful, they have held the blacks in degradation or in slavery; wherever the Negroes have been strongest,

---

[73] *Id.* at 220.

[74] *Id.* at 203 (The black race are "told from infancy that [their] race is naturally inferior to that of the whites, [so] he assents to the proposition and is ashamed of his own nature").

[75] *Id.* at 247.

[76] *Id.* at 248 ("I reserve my execration for those who, after a thousand years of freedom, brought back slavery into the world once more").

[77] *Id.* at 221 ("Christianity suppressed slavery, but the Christians of the sixteenth century re-established it").

[78] *Id.* ("[T]he most formidable of all the ills that threaten the future of the Union arises from the presence of a black population upon its territory.").

[79] *Id.* at 539.

they have destroyed the whites: this has been the only balance that has ever taken place between the two races.[80]

The resurrection of slavery by the British in the sixteenth century was fully against the traditional natural law. Pope Paul III in his bull *Sublimus Dei* had already condemned slavery based on a long track of human experience, which had shown that even from an economic viewpoint, slavery was non-conducive to progress.[81]

For De Tocqueville, even the abolishment of slavery would prove to be troublesome. In fact, he noticed that the former slave "transmits the eternal mark of his ignominy to all his descendants; and although the law may abolish slavery, God alone can obliterate the traces of its existence".[82] Also, on the part of former enslavers, a "natural prejudice [would arise prompting them] to despise whoever has been their inferior long after he has become their equal,"[83] founded on the perception that, "as we are legally equal, I treat you worst less we be confounded together".[84]

In sum, once slavery is introduced in a society —as the British did in North America— the differences between the races are only perpetuated but in different manners, even after slavery is legally abolished:

slave states scorn "not only labor but all the undertakings that labor promotes; as he lives in an idle independence, his tastes are those of an idle man; money has lost a portion of its value in his eyes; he covets wealth much less than pleasure and excitement ... [and they develop a] passionate love of field sports and military exercises; he delights in violent bodily exertion ... Thus slavery prevents the whites not only from becoming opulent, but even from desiring to become so [and there is a] striking difference between the commercial capacity of the inhabitants of the South and those of the North. At the present day it is only the Northern states that are in possession of shipping, manufactures, railroads, and canals.[85]

---

[80]   *Id.* at 223-4.

[81]   *Id.* at 228 (recognizing that "[t]he free workman is paid, but he does his work quicker than the slave; and rapidity of execution is one of the great elements of economy [...] but in the end the slave has cost more than the free servant, and his labor is less productive").

[82]   *Id.* at 222.

[83]   *Id.*

[84]   *Id.* at 225.

[85]   *Id.* at 229.

B. *Tendency to Uniformity*

De Tocqueville saw that the passion for equality amongst Americans inescapably led to uniformity in ideas, manners, and mores.[86] He regretted that the American equalizing society[87] produced "so few ignorant and at the same time so few learned individuals".[88] He was far from celebrating such order of things: "the sight of such universal uniformity saddens and chills me and I am tempted to regret that state of society which has ceased to be".[89]

C. *Idolization of Equality*

De Tocqueville raised red flags against the abstract principle of equality embedded in the American version of the 'natural rights' theory. While he recognized that the principle of equality was "the supreme law of democratic societies,"[90] he also noticed that "among the Americans it is freedom that is old; equality is of comparatively modern date".[91]

However, the contours of the idea of "equality" were never fully formulated at the onset of the American republic. This led De Tocqueville to state that Americans "cannot understand why a rule that is applicable to one man should not be equally applicable to all others".[92]

Obviously, this unsophisticated proposal of equality created many dangers to personal freedoms in the United States.[93] The reason is that the abstract and undefined concept of equality embedded ideas contrary to the traditional natural law, namely:

---

[86] *Id.* at 505 ("[W]hen the equality of conditions is long established and complete, as all men [and Americans] copy from one another [and] speak or act in the same manner").

[87] *Id.* at 513 (in America "all men are alike and do things pretty nearly alike.").

[88] *Id.* at 43.

[89] *Id.* at 601.

[90] *Id.* at 528.

[91] *Id.* at 564.

[92] *Id.* at 556.

[93] *Id.* at 597.

(a) Equality disregards that nature is unequal:[94] for example, man cannot alter the uneven distribution of intellectual talents amongst God's creatures.[95]

(b) Equality creates frustration in citizens because it can never be perfectly achieved.[96] In fact, equality "suggests to the Americans the idea of the indefinite perfectibility of man,"[97] which is an altogether unreachable goal.

(c) Since in equalizing societies men "commonly seek for the sources of truth in themselves or in those who are like themselves,"[98] they show contempt toward talent, authority,[99] and equality ends up transforming the minimum social denominator into the common social denominator.[100]

(d) Equality fosters distrust among men: this is the logical consequence of every man's opinion having the same value as any other man's.[101]

(e) Common opinion is formed by standardized appreciations of the greater number of people,[102] and is not necessarily connected to the truth. Moreover, equality unleashes untried and willful philosophical ideas not necessarily connected with reality.

(f) Equality relativizes religion. As De Tocqueville pointed out:

Everybody there adopts great numbers of theories, on philosophy, morals, and politics, without inquiry, upon public trust; and if we examine it very closely, it will be perceived that religion itself holds sway there much less as a doctrine of revelation than as a commonly received opinion.[103]

---

[94]   *Id.* at 303 ("there are in nature no beings exactly alike").

[95]   *Id.* at 44 ("The gifts of intellect proceed directly from God, and man cannot prevent their unequal distribution").

[96]   *Id.* at 108 ("Democratic institutions awaken and foster a passion for equality which they can never entirely satisfy").

[97]   *Id.* at 324.

[98]   *Id.* at 300.

[99]   *Id.* at 550 ("the great social equality which prevails in democracies ultimately renders the private soldier independent of the officer and thus destroys the bond of discipline. This is a mistake").

[100]   *Id.* at 327 ("in few of the civilized nations of our time have the higher sciences made less progress than in the United States; and in few have great artists, distinguished poets, or celebrated writers [and this is a] natural and inevitable result of equality").

[101]   *Id.* at 300 ("[a]t periods of equality men have no faith in one another").

[102]   *Id.* at 301 ("the greater truth should go with the greater number").

[103]   *Id.*

(g) Equality brings about intolerance. Counterintuitively, there is an innate trend in equality toward the prohibition of dissent,[104] that is, a trend toward tyranny.

(h) As equality increases the private egos, it consequentially fosters individualism and consumerism.[105] Unlike egoism, which is an "exaggerated love of self," individualism is "a mature and calm feeling [and] is of democratic origin".[106]

(i) As equality drowns talent, it weakens men and makes societies more vulnerable to foreign aggressions, and therefore, it threatens the independence of the people.[107]

(j) Equality discourages the arts.[108]

(k) Equality creates an inordinate zeal in men,[109] superior even to the passion for freedom.[110] This caused De Tocqueville to observe that, " the desire of equality always becomes more insatiable in proportion as equality is more complete".[111]

(l) Equality creates enduring negative effects in society that are "slowly disclosed,"[112] and difficult to correct.[113]

(m) Gender equalization tends to the slow destruction of society. De Tocqueville pointed out that, "attempting to make one sex equal to the

---

[104] *Id.* at 302 ("[i]n the principle of equality I very clearly discern two tendencies; one leading the mind of every man to untried thoughts, the other prohibiting him from thinking at all").

[105] *Id.* at 313 ("[i]t tends to isolate [men] from one another, to concentrate every man's attention upon himself; and it lays open the soul to an inordinate love of material gratification.").

[106] *Id.* at 395.

[107] *Id.* at 45 ("in a state where the citizens are all practically equal, it becomes difficult for them to preserve their independence against the aggressions of power").

[108] *Id.* at 367 ("the principle of equality ... has dried up most of the old springs of poetry").

[109] *Id.* at 393 ("[t]he passion that equality creates must therefore be at once strong and general [and] the passion for equality penetrates on every side into men's hearts").

[110] *Id.* at 390.

[111] *Id.* at 433.

[112] *Id.* at 393.

[113] *Id.* at 392 ("none but attentive and clear-sighted men perceive the perils with which equality threatens us ... the calamities ... that they will only fall upon future generations.").

120

other, both are degraded [and] nothing could ever result but weak men and disorderly women".[114]

It is "powerful private individuals whom the equality of conditions has swept away"[115] who are the main movers of the equalizing movement. As members of the community "become more equal, become more ignorant and coarse, it is difficult to foresee to what pitch of stupid excesses their selfishness may lead them".[116]

The only social remedy against extreme equalization in society is the fight for political freedom,[117] or else as De Tocqueville prophetically stated in the very last paragraph of his book "*Democracy in America*,"

> The nations of our time cannot prevent the conditions of men from becoming equal, but it depends upon themselves whether the principle of equality is to lead them to servitude or freedom, to knowledge or barbarism, to prosperity or wretchedness.[118]

D. *Rejection of Tradition*

The most telling characteristic of Protestantism is its rejection of tradition as an authoritative source of knowledge and human rule.[119] The mental attitude behind this rejection is the recognition of one's "own reason as the most obvious and proximate source of truth".[120] The prideful attitude generated by equality in the form of independence of mind[121] leads to a condemnation of forms,[122] and to the denial of anything that cannot be comprehended. This denial, in turn, leaves "little faith for whatever is extraordinary and an almost insurmountable distaste for whatever is supernatural".[123]

---

[114] *Id.* at 497.

[115] *Id.* at 407.

[116] *Id.* at 417.

[117] *Id.* at 402.

[118] *Id.* at 603.

[119] *Id.* at 376 (Americans "accept tradition only as a means of information.").

[120] *Id.* at 295.

[121] *Id.* at 297.

[122] *Id.* at 296.

[123] *Id.*

A second aspect implicit in this rejection is a vague notion said to be of limitlessness in the abilities of the human mind, that is, that the human intellect is able to explore, apprehend, and ultimately master all phenomena.[124]

Reality, on the opposite side –as guided by the traditional natural law– shows that societies exist when they hold common beliefs and consents "on certain matters of belief already formed".[125] In fact, it is simply not possible for everyone to inquire into every phenomena occurring around, and to form one's own opinion based on such inquiry. Man, accordingly, must form his mind and convince his spirit about things in many occasions on what others[126] have witnessed, demonstrated, experienced, or lived previously in history.[127] All this accumulated knowledge and experience of mankind is called "tradition," which the 'natural rights' theory so strongly rejected, to the detriment of Western societies.

This attitude toward tradition does not constitute subservience to a remote past or to dead ideas of other times. Quite the contrary, this mind-set reveals a "salutary servitude, which allows [men] to make a good use of freedom".[128] Ultimately, a necessary instrument to keeping the role of tradition must exist, and this is the 'principle of authority,' which "must then always occur ... in some part or other of the moral and intellectual world".[129]

E. *The Principle of Absolute Majoritarianis*

The "omnipotence of the majority"[130] is another danger stemming from a concept of political power conceived away from the traditional natural law. De Tocqueville warned that in the nascent American republic "the

---

[124]   *Id.* (alluding that American Protestantism "readily conclude(s) that everything in the world may be explained, and that nothing in it transcends the limits of the understanding").

[125]   *Id.* at 298.

[126]   *Id.* at 299 (referring to what "men of greater ability have found out").

[127]   *Id.*

[128]   *Id.*

[129]   *Id.*

[130]   *Id.* at 104.

power of the majority [was] so absolute and irresistible,"[131] as to constitute the "very essence of democratic government".[132]

In the American model founded over the 'natural rights' theory, the absolute sovereignty of the majority was not only political, but also moral, and was:

> based upon the notion that there is more intelligence and wisdom in a number of men united than in a single individual, and that the number of the legislators is more important than their quality. The theory of equality is applied to the intellects of men.[133]

De Tocqueville found that the principle of absolute majoritarianism was a "detestable maxim [since it proposed that] people have a right to do anything".[134] He alerted that majoritarianism causes self-complacency[135] and was "favorable to the legal despotism of the legislature".[136] He also warned that the political axiom of majoritarianism was prone to raise "formidable barriers around the liberty of opinion,"[137] and would expose dissenters to "continued obloquy and persecution".[138] In a stark assertion, De Tocqueville warned the despotism[139] created by majoritarianism would ultimately lead to anarchy.[140] This fear was not unwarranted, since Thomas Jefferson had also warned that, "[t]he tyranny of the legislature is really the danger most to be feared ... [t]he tyranny of the executive power will come in its turn, but at a more distant period".[141]

Against the backdrop of the absolute majoritarianism proposed by the 'natural rights' theory, traditional natural law had long taught that "God

---

[131] *Id.* at 156.

[132] *Id.* at 145.

[133] *Id.* at 146.

[134] *Id.* at 148.

[135] *Id.* at 155 ("[t]he majority lives in the perpetual utterance of self-applause").

[136] *Id.* at 151.

[137] *Id.* at 152.

[138] *Id.* at 153.

[139] *Id.* at 198 ("if the peaceable dominion of the majority is not founded among us in time, we shall sooner or later fall under the unlimited authority of a single man").

[140] *Id.* at 157 ("[i]f ever the free institutions of America are destroyed, that event may be attributed to the omnipotence of the majority ... anarchy will then be the result ... brought about by despotism").

[141] *Id.* at 158.

alone can be omnipotent,"[142] and that moral values –such as "humanity, justice, and reason; and in the political world, vested rights"[143]— are of a superior rank to majorities.

F. Loss of Religion and Moral Breakdown of the American Democratic Experiment

Once the European aristocratic privileges were left behind, property evenly divided, and education broadly available, "the desire of acquiring the comforts of the world"[144] expanded to all social classes. As the American experiment is essentially an enterprise of the middle class,[145] this class grew in to what today are known as materialistic and consumerist attitudes.

As a backdrop, De Tocqueville saw that "Americans are a very religious people,"[146] that they founded their political institutions based on their religious ideals,[147] and that their faith constituted a strong wall against the antagonistic desires of political majoritarianism.[148]

However, the negative tendencies present in the human soul slowly started to arise in the American political experience. In his hour, De Tocqueville noticed that religion had started to lose "its empire over the souls of men [and that] the most prominent boundary that divided good from evil"[149] started to become overthrown thus yielding to despotism and license. In sum, the lax morality that early on began to make inroads into the American society was the result of the loss of religion in the people.[150]

---

[142] *Id.* at 149.

[143] *Id.* at 277.

[144] *Id.* at 423.

[145] *Id.* at 424 ("the passion for physical comforts is essentially a passion of the middle classes.").

[146] *Id.* at 486.

[147] *Id.* at 440.

[148] *Id.* at 317.

[149] *Id.* at 197.

[150] *Id.* at 79 ("[G]reat wealth and extreme poverty, capital cities of large size, a lax morality, selfishness, and antagonism of interests are the dangers.").

G. *Awakening of Disordered Passions*

De Tocqueville detected that the zealous desire for equality immersed in the American democratic experiment generated distrust in the general people toward distinguished citizens.[151] As a result, the most able citizens "retire from the political arena".[152]

Another perhaps unintended effect of the equalization brought about by the 'natural rights' theory is the "unbounded desire of riches, and an excessive love of independence as propensities very dangerous to society".[153] The rejection of tradition is accompanied by the feeling that society is to be reinvented in every generation. De Tocqueville comments that as every man forgets his ancestors, eventually he is confined in the "solitude of his own heart".[154]

De Tocqueville also identifies self-centeredness of the Protestant cultural ethos[155] existing in American society, about which he wrote:

> He who has set his heart exclusively upon the pursuit of worldly welfare is always in a hurry, for he has but a limited time at his disposal to reach, to grasp, and to enjoy it. The recollection of the shortness of life is a constant spur to him. Besides the good things that he possesses, he every instant fancies a thousand others that death will prevent him from trying if he does not try, them soon. This thought fills him with anxiety, fear and regret and keeps his mind in ceaseless trepidation, which leads him perpetually to change his plans and his abode.[156]

In definitive, one of the most notorious, and pervasive effects of equalization in the American society was –according to De Tocqueville– "in the midst of the instability of everything [is the instability of] the heart of man".[157]

---

[151] *Id.* at 108 ("democratic institutions strongly tend to promote the feeling of envy in the human heart.").

[152] *Id.* at 109.

[153] *Id.* at 177.

[154] *Id.* at 397.

[155] *Id.* at 438 (expressing that the chief business of Americans "is to secure for themselves a government which will allow them to acquire the things they covet and which will not debar them from the peaceful enjoyment of those possessions which they have already acquired").

[156] *Id.* at 431.

[157] *Id.* at 473.

H. *Mediocrity of Elected Officials and of the People in General*

A son of aristocratic France, De Tocqueville had little patience with what he saw in American society concerning the social disregard for hereditary or earned merit[158] and for the constant pursuit of gain.[159] Indeed, he states that,

> The men who are entrusted with the direction of public affairs in the United States are frequently inferior, in both capacity and morality, to those whom an aristocracy would raise to power.[160]

He was particularly adamant about the loss of beauty and art created by the practicality of the American equalizing mind.[161] De Tocqueville saw that this general apathy or hostility toward beauty was present in letters,[162] literature,[163] drama,[164] and even the English language spoken by Americans was infested with "new words [that] are more especially taken from the jargon of parties, the mechanical arts, or the language of trade".[165]

The original cause of these maladies were found in the rejection of tradition. In particular, the dismissal of erudition in American society was very hard for Tocqueville to come to terms with.[166] For him, the general disregard for good taste bordered with the unacceptable.[167]

---

[158] *Id.* at 338 ("[I]n aristocratic ages science is more particularly called upon to furnish gratification to the mind; in democracies, to the body").

[159] *Id.* at 334 ("[E]veryone is in motion, some in quest of power, others of gain").

[160] *Id.* at 132.

[161] *Id.* at 340 (saying that Americans "habitually prefer the useful to the beautiful").

[162] *Id.* at 352 ("[A]s the time they can devote to letters is very short, they seek to make the best use of the whole of it. They prefer books which may be easily procured, quickly read, and which require no learned researches to be understood").

[163] *Id.* at 352 ("…literature is always infested with a tribe of writers who look upon letters as a mere trade").

[164] *Id.* at 352 ("[T]he object of authors will be to astonish rather than to please, and to stir the passions more than to charm the taste").

[165] *Id.* at 358.

[166] *Id.* at 294 (asserting that American society held "erudition very cheap and care but little for what occurred at Rome and Athens; they want to hear something that concerns themselves, and the delineation of the present age is what they demand.").

[167] *Id.* at 111 ("[O]n entering the House of Representatives at Washington, one is struck by the vulgar demeanor of that great assembly … the only reason … is that it is … elected by the people directly").

I. *Instability Caused by Periodic Elections*

De Tocqueville saw that the political debate in American society was periodically settled in never-ending elections.[168] Permanent election cycles, in his view, prevented a "consistent policy" and thus brought instability to the country.[169]

J. *Patriotism as a Fleeting Sentiment*

Tocqueville says that the word 'patriotism' itself is not of very ancient date in the language".[170] In fact, the history and tradition of political allegiances in the Western world pivot around lordships of one man over a determined group of people. The concept of the nation-state is of recent origin in the context of Western history.

Therefore, patriotism emerged as the sentiment expressing the loyalty and attachment that a particular individual feels toward a specific political unity located in a determined physical territory, called 'the State.' Patriotism is directed to the State, but is oftentimes "a mere extension of individual selfishness,"[171] and "like all instinctive passions ... incites great transient exertions, but no continuity of effort".[172]

De Tocqueville feared that the transiency of the patriotic feeling was not enough to hold the American Union indissoluble. In fact, he added that,

> If one of the states chose to withdraw its name from the contract [the Union], it would be difficult to disprove its right of doing so, and the Federal government would have no means of maintaining its claims directly, either by force or by right.[173]

Again, he added that,

> if any portion of the Union seriously desired to separate itself from the other states, they would not be able, nor indeed would they attempt, to prevent it; and

---

[168]   *Id.* at 112 ("[W]hen elections occur frequently, their recurrence keeps society in a feverish excitement and gives a continual instability to public affairs").

[169]   *Id.* at 113.

[170]   *Id.* at 517.

[171]   *Id.* at 251.

[172]   *Id.* at 134.

[173]   *Id.* at 253.

that the present Union will last only as long as the states which compose it choose to continue members of the confederation.[174]

K. *Emergence of an Aristocratic Class*

Another risk inherent in the American equalizing experiment perceived by De Tocqueville was the surfacing of a "manufacturing aristocracy [as] one of the harshest that ever existed in the world".[175] With the appearance of this newly enriched American elite, "inequality increases".[176] Then, equality shows that inequality is its logical and natural result.

L. *Growth of the Central Government*

De Tocqueville predicted that, "centralization will be the natural government"[177] of the United States of America. Concentration of power would increase amongst Americans "in the same proportion as their equality".[178]

In a society where competition and the pursuit of profit go undeterred,[179] such as the United States, it is difficult for citizens to create enduring bonds of trust. Therefore, the State "alone inspires private individuals with confidence, because the state alone appears to be endowed with strength and durability".[180] Naturally, then, the State –around which all wealth flows– assumes roles that were formerly the province of private individuals or associations,[181] as it happened in times when –under tradi-

---

[174]   *Id.* at 253.

[175]   *Id.* at 454.

[176]   *Id.* at 452.

[177]   *Id.* at 562.

[178]   *Id.* at 566.

[179]   *Id.* at 583 (saying that there is "an innumerable multitude of men, all equal and alike, incessantly endeavoring to procure the petty and paltry pleasures with which they glut their lives. Each them, living apart, is as a stranger to the of all rest").

[180]   *Id.* at 573.

[181]   *Id.* at 571 ("[T]he state almost exclusively undertakes to supply bread to the hungry, assistance and shelter to the sick, work to the idle, and to act as the sole reliever of all kinds of misery").

tional natural law– the economy was ruled according to the principle of subsidiariety.[182] As De Tocqueville recognized,

> [a]lmost all the charitable establishments of Europe were formerly in the hands of private persons or of guilds; they are now almost all dependent on the supreme government.[183]

The principle of equality would facilitate the installation of an absolute and despotic regime as a consequence of the uniformity of their appreciations. In other words, if the majority of the country decided to have a despotic regime –De Tocqueville reflected– there was no way to stop the feelings of such majority.[184] He fatefully foretold that despotism coupled with "heavy taxation, might eventually compromise the fate of republican institutions".[185]

The "soft" unprecedented[186] installation of tyranny in the United States would appear "with some of the outward forms of freedom, and that it might even establish itself under the wing of the sovereignty of the people".[187] But in De Tocqueville's reasoning, the "yoke of a centralized administration"[188] would not operate as an outwardly destructive, tyrannical power, but rather as a sort of compression over the people which would extinguish it slowly. Finally reducing it "to nothing better than a flock of timid and industrious animals, of which the government is the shepherd".[189]

The ultimate tyrannical phase of the equalizing religion professed by the followers of the 'natural rights' theory would be their dominion over religion: the "Catholic as well as Protestant, religion is in danger of falling into the hands of the government".[190] At the pinnacle of his prophetic ut-

---

[182] Edmund Burke, *Speech on Economic Reform* (February 1780), *in* Rogers, *supra note* 18, at 249 ("commerce ... flourishes most when it is left to itself").

[183] Alexis de Tocqueville, supra *note* 504, at 570-1.

[184] *Id.* at 585 (commenting that Americans "combine the principle of equality and that of popular sovereignty [and] they console themselves for being in tutelage by the reflection that they have chosen their own guardians").

[185] *Id.* at 276.

[186] *Id.* at 583 ("the species of oppression by which democratic nations are menaced is unlike anything that ever before existed in the world").

[187] *Id.* at 585.

[188] *Id.* at 70.

[189] *Id.* at 584-5.

[190] *Id.* at 571.

terances, De Tocqueville foresaw that equalization would sooner of later lead to the persecution of the Christian religion: "the nations of Christendom would perhaps eventually undergo some oppression like that which hung over several of the nations of the ancient world".[191]

Finally, De Tocqueville clearly saw that all these calamities would befall on the United States as a direct consequence of the 'natural rights' theory principle of equality, which had "prepared men for these things".[192] His call to awareness still resonates today, as embodied in his statement that:

> in the present democratic times that the true friends of the liberty and the greatness of man ought constantly to be on the alert to prevent the power of government from lightly sacrificing the private rights of individuals to general execution of its designs.[193]

---

[191] *Id.* at 581.

[192] *Id.* at 584.

[193] *Id.* at 594.

CHAPTER VII:

SEARCHING FOR THE NATURAL LAW NOTIONS THAT INSPIRED THE FOUNDING FATHERS

1. *In General*

As it has been extensively demonstrated in this work, the "natural rights" theory is but a distortion of the traditional natural law doctrine whose systematic elaboration was first magnificently presented in the Western world by St. Thomas of Aquinas, and elaborated later by the Spanish Scholastics.

Even after the beginning of the religiously motivated historical distortion of the traditional natural law in the sixteenth century, the truth of it was retained by the 'natural rights' theory and provided a background for the natural law thinking of the Founding Fathers. The distorted natural law theory retained by them had a strong degree of truth in several notions: (1) that human rights are God-given rights which are prior to society and government; (2) that human rights are merely declared through positive law, *i.e.*, by the Constitution and legislation; (3) that human rights are inalienable; (3) that the whole purpose of government is to protect those rights; and (4) that citizens preserve in all times their right to rebel against positive law that does not conform to natural law.

The principal distortion of the 'natural rights' theory was the appropriation of the main aspects of the traditional natural law doctrine's main predicaments, with the consequent repudiation of several other predicaments, such as the principle that natural law derives from divine law. The Deists watered down the Judeo-Christian God for concepts such "divinity" or "Providence". In a sense, the 'natural rights' theory was a rebellion against God.

2. *On the Contours of the Idea of Liberty for the Founding Fathers*

The topic of whether the Founding Fathers were aware of or followed traditional natural law is not without controversy. The historical context within which the American Independence movement took place was one where "the state-of-nature or modern natural rights analysis appears to have been the dominant theoretical justification for revolution and written constitutions".[1] More precisely, "natural rights were understood to be subject to natural law"[2] during the Independence period.

On one side, there is the widespread –and to a certain point predominant– notion that "natural rights and natural law are not only suggestive but also indeterminate-ideas ... often used to legitimate what are, in fact, our individual preconceptions and desires".[3] But even *arguendo* that that has been the case since the foundation of the American republic, history and reality show that the Founding Fathers did embrace natural law principles, though with "substantial differences"[4] amongst them.

In effect, for one sector of the Framers, natural law was considered as a "law of human nature and as the foundation of moral rules,"[5] and consisted mainly of "prudential rules of noninjurious behavior derivable from principles of equal freedom and self-preservation".[6] Key among these natural law principles was the most cherished of all to the Founders: the principle of natural liberty.[7] To sacrifice it "to government in a written constitution" was thought to be the kernel of what the whole edifice of natural law was about. In other words, the "limited version" of natural law (based almost exclusively on the principle of liberty to the detriment of other natural law principles) was for one sector of the Framers intimately connected with the principle of self-preservation. In accordance with this principle, early Americans:

---

[1]   Philip A. Hamburger, *Natural Rights, Natural Law, and American Constitutions*, 102 Yale L.J. 907 (1993), at 939.

[2]   *Id.* at 954.

[3]   *Id.* at 907.

[4]   *Id.* at 926.

[5]   *Id.* at 924.

[6]   *Id.* at 926.

[7]   Patrick Henry Center for Individual Liberty, *Patrick Henry's Speeches*, *available at* http://www.patrickhenrycenter.com/Speeches.aspx (quoting Henry's famous 1778 "give me liberty or give me death" speech at the Virginia Ratifying Convention).

sacrificed a portion of their natural liberty to civil government; they gave up some natural liberty in order to enable government to preserve the residue, a sacrifice accomplished by means of a constitution or contract of fundamental law.[8]

On the other spectrum –as Professor Robert Barker of Duquesne has of late noted– when in 1776 the Founding Fathers declared the Independence of the United States, they invoked *"the Laws of Nature and of Nature's God"*.[9] He subsequently asserts –and rightly so– that

> [t]here can be no doubt that those delegates in Philadelphia who adopted that Declaration believed in, and, based the nation's independence on, the Natural Law; that is, that God, in creating the universe, implanted in the nature of man a body of Law to which all human beings are subject, which is superior to all manmade law, and which is knowable by human reason".[10]

Undoubtedly, as a legal instrument, the U.S. Constitution was not designed to express juridical philosophies but rather to establish a form of government, and to guarantee the rights and freedoms of the American people. However, as Professor Barker teaches, one of the most striking characteristics of the U.S. Constitution is that it embodied "clear and admirable applications of the Natural Law".[11] In addition, Professor Barker has advanced a strikingly veritable proposal by observing that, "the dominant philosophical influence upon the Founders was that of classical-traditional Natural Law".[12]

Barker's findings have been decidedly corroborated by another American academic in recent times explaining that, "virtually everyone of those Framers [...] acknowledged the principles of natural law and natural rights".[13] Moreover, at the beginning of the American Republic, both "Federalists and Anti-Federalists agreed that American society widely understood and respected the premises of natural law".[14] The original documents of the American independence (the "Declaration of Independ-

---

[8] Hamburger, *supra note* 763, at 956.

[9] Robert S. Barker, *Natural Law and the United States Constitution*, The Review of Metaphysics 66 (September 2012), at 105.

[10] *Id.* at 105.

[11] *Id.* at 106.

[12] *Id.* at 113.

[13] Terry Brennan, *Natural Rights and the Constitution: the Original "Original Intent*," 15 Harv. J.L. & Pub. Pol'y 965 (1992), at 971-2.

[14] *Id.* at 973.

ence" and the "Resolves of the First Continental Congress")[15] *and* the "text and debates of the ratification era show that the founding generation almost universally accepted natural law".[16] The most important Founding Fathers (George Washington, Alexander Hamilton, John Adams, John Dikinson, Patrick Henry, George Mason, James Wilson, and Thomas Jefferson, among other) unequivocally resorted to natural law as a foundation of their ideas about government and democracy. Another logical result of the acceptance of natural law by the Framers was that "natural rights were superior to positive law and the Constitution".[17]

The right to resist oppression was chief amongst the natural rights of the people recognized by the Framers; a right that "can never be alienated".[18] In this sense, the basic natural law ideas on the right of rebellion professed by the Founding Fathers are in full harmony with the Thomistic teaching on the matter. Little room was left for Paine's and Bentham's ideas amongst the Founding Fathers, and the records strongly leans on the side of their rejection.

As attested by the historical record discretely reviewed above, the Founding Fathers, in general, had a correct understanding of natural law, particularly, of traditional natural law, as explained by many of their assumptions concerning the principles of government, subsidiariety, liberty, the right of rebellion, the legitimacy of positive law, and the basic rights of the citizens. In that sense, undoubtedly, the Framers followed traditional natural law.[19]

Despite this historic evidence, the discussion about the reception or recognition of natural law by the U.S. Constitution still pervades current legal debates in the United States. For example, the interpretation of the Ninth Amendment to the U.S. Constitution[20] is one of the chief constitu-

---

[15] *Id.* at 974.

[16] *Id.* at 975.

[17] *Id.* at 969. *Id.* at 978 ("[P]ositive law may declare and affirm these rights, but it cannot confer them").

[18] *Id.* at 979.

[19] Hamburger, *supra note* 763, at 937 (indicating that, "[W]hen Americans said that constitutions and other civil laws should be drafted to reflect the principles of natural law, they were building upon the medieval tradition that lawmakers should formulate civil laws in accordance with natural law").

[20] The National Archives, *The Charters of Freedom: A New World is at Hand, available at* http://www.archives.gov/exhibits/charters/constitution.html (Ninth Amendment: "[T]he enumeration in the Constitution, of certain rights, shall not be construed to deny or disparage others retained by the people").

tional areas where heated discussions about the reach of natural law and the U.S. Constitution still occur. In particular, a doctrinal constitutional trend called "originalism" seeks to find the central rule of constitutional interpretation in the "will" of the Founding Fathers *as expressed* in the Constitution. In other words, in light of the Ninth Amendment, originalists reject all judicial attempts to "smuggle 'natural law' and 'natural rights' concepts into the Constitution"[21] as alleged "unenumerated natural rights".[22] Notwithstanding these misgivings toward natural law, the historical record proofs that it was the "will" of the Founding Fathers not to enumerate natural rights into the text of the Constitution. In fact, it was expressly recognized that including a rigid list of natural rights would create the insurmountable risk of precluding other rights about which the American society would become aware[23] during its future civic life.[24] Hence, the "open" language used by the Ninth Amendment referring to "inalienable rights [that] would be retained without enumeration".[25] In sum, for the Framers unenumerated rights were natural rights and "did not require textual recognition,"[26] in congruence with the teachings of traditional natural law.

3. *The Founding Fathers and their Idea of Natural Law*

The Protestant religion, under its myriad of expressions, was predominant in most of the provinces of North America.[27] Save for two exceptions,[28] all of the Founding Fathers were Protestant in religion.[29] Protes-

---

[21]   Brennan, *supra note* 775, at 993.

[22]   *Id.* at 992.

[23]   *Id.* at 1006 (stating that "William Penn" agreed that the full array of natural rights was "unfortunately not yet known" to Americans").

[24]   *Id.* at 1002-5 (referring to the right of self-government; the right to resist or abolish government; the right of conscientious objection; the right to fish, fowl, and game; the freedom of information and inquiry; the prohibition of certain monopolies; the rights of navigation, emigration and travel; the right to a healthy environment; the right to privacy; the right of political and economic asylum; the right to extended limited protection to employees, women, children, and the mentally incompetent; and the prohibition of cruelty against animals).

[25]   *Id.* at 995.

[26]   *Id.* at 1008.

[27]   Burke, *supra note* 310, at 187.

[28]   John Dickinson of Delaware and Daniel Carroll of Maryland (alluded to in Barker, *supra note* 771, at 111.

tantism agreed "in nothing but in the communion of the spirit of liberty".[30] Edmund Burke noticed that this fierce spirit of liberty was "stronger in the English colonies probably than in any other people of the earth".[31] Now, the frenzy for liberty present in the American experiment concealed, ultimately, a "desire and design of a tyrannick domination".[32] On the other hand, a large majority of the representatives that participated in the Continental Congress were lawyers.[33]

Contrary to the desires of unlimited liberty professed by the American followers of the 'natural rights' theory, traditional natural law –as explained, for example, by Edmund Burke– always knew how to "distinguish between true and false liberty".[34] True liberty cannot be separated from "order and virtue [and] cannot exist at all without them".[35]

Despite the un-orthodox views of traditional natural law that might have pervaded the Constitutional Convention, three important principles of that discipline found their way in the definitional framework of the U.S. Constitution: the principle of limited government, the principle of subsidiarity, and the approach that the "guaranteeing of traditional rights [is to be enforced only] against government".[36]

4. *The Views of James Madison, Thomas Jefferson and Alexander Hamilton on Natural Law*

The Father of the U.S. Constitution, James Madison, wrote about the duty that man owes to God as, "precedent, both in order of time and in

---

[29] Burke, *supra note* 310, at 187 (["a]ll Protestantism, even the most cold and passive, is a sort of dissent").

[30] *Id.*

[31] *Id.* at 186.

[32] Burke, *An Appeal from the New to the Old Whigs in Consequence of Some Late Discussions in Parliament, Relative to the Reflections on the French Revolution, supra note* 190, at 507.

[33] Burke, *supra note* 310, at 188.

[34] Burke, An *Appeal from the New to the Old Whigs in Consequence of Some Late Discussions in Parliament, Relative to the Reflections on the French Revolution, supra note* 190, at 535.

[35] *Id.* at 502.

[36] Barker, *supra note* 771, at 114.

degree of obligation, to the claims of Civil Society".[37] Alexander Hamilton was even more explicit about natural law as the source of all human law when he declared that it,

> has constituted an eternal and immutable law, which is indispensably obligatory upon all mankind, prior to any human institution whatever. This is what is called the law of nature....[38]

Jefferson's religious and political ideas "responded, in part, to a Puritan legacy".[39] He, for example, "steered America away from the Winthropian aspiration to be a "model of Christian charity[40] "a beacon lit upon a hill".[41] He recognized in his day how, in a great manner, Christianity was the foundation of common law. Specifically, he exemplified this by identifying the conducts punished by Christianity, which were also criminalized by British common law since ancient times.[42]

Jefferson's famous reference to the "laws of nature"[43] in his draft of the Declaration of Independence was used as a ground for the American colonies to throw off the yoke of subordination. This instance shows his conviction about the existence of a natural law system prior and superior to positive law – which this latter may not legitimately contradict.

Based on those "laws of nature" Jefferson –who was raised an Anglican[44] but who, "to the end ... remained more of an Enlightenment deist than a traditional Christian"[45]– recognized certain "truths" that we may accurately call 'natural rights': (1) that "all men are created equal,"[46] that

---

[37] James Madison, "Memorial and Remonstrance Against Religious Assessments, June 20, 1785," *in* The Founders' Constitution, vol. 5, ed. Philip B. Kurland and Ralph Lerner (Indianapolis: Liberty Fund, 1987), 82, *cited* in Barker, supra note 771, at 109.

[38] *Id.*

[39] Holland, *supra note* 572, 85.

[40] *Id.* at 87.

[41] Alexis de Tocqueville, supra *note* 504, at 27.

[42] Thomas Jefferson, Report of Cases Determined in the General Court of Virginia from 1730 to 1740 and From 1768, to 1772 (Charlottesville, F. Carr, and Co., 1829), at 141-142 ("the whole Bible and Testament, in a lump, make a part of the common law of the land...").

[43] Holland, *supra note* 572, at 87.

[44] *Id.* at 89.

[45] *Id.* at 90.

[46] The National Archives, Declaration of Independence (July 4, 1776), http://www.archives.gov/exhibits/charters/declaration_transcript.html.

is, as "no natural political authority exists, all men are naturally free to govern themselves;"[47] (2) that all men are "endowed with certain inalienable rights, including life, liberty, and the pursuit of happiness;"[48] (3) that the whole purpose of government is to "'secure' the free and safe exercise of these 'inherent' rights;[49] and (4) that the "just powers [of the government derive] from the consent of the governed".[50]

Further evidence of the "simple morality of [the] natural rights"[51] ideology adopted by the Founding Fathers, and which stemmed from Jefferson's ideas, is found in the following aspects: (1) that one's morality is as good and legitimate as anybody else's; (2) that the existence of a "foundational public morality"[52] remains impossible under this scheme of things; and (3) that, as a consequence, social consensus is not only necessary to justify social life, but is erected as the ultimate basis of political life, legislation, and of public morality in society.

Notwithstanding the imperfect notion of Christianity to which Jefferson adhered, it retained some strength as evidenced in the "Christian concept of charity," which was the cornerstone for Jefferson's notion of the "public morality of natural rights".[53]

5. *The "Pursuit of Happiness"*
Aim of the U.S. Declaration of Independence[54]

At some point in his life, Thomas Jefferson said, "I too am an Epicurean".[55] However, the amalgam resulting of his early Epicureanism with Christian beliefs produced "his view of Christian charity ... as essential to America's national happiness".[56] His reference to "the circle of our felici-

---

47   Holland, *supra note* 572, at 88.
48   U.S. Declaration of Independence.
49   Holland, *supra note* 572, at 88.
50   *Id.* at 88.
51   *Id.* at 89.
52   *Id.*
53   *Id.* at 95.
54   U.S. Declaration of Independence.
55   Holland, *supra note* 572, at 89.
56   *Id.* at 93.

ties"[57] also shows the sturdiness of his conviction in the principle of happiness. He even listed two 'blessings' which he considered 'essential to national happiness.' One of these blessings was "allegiance to 'republican principles,'" that is, the principles of public morality and natural rights".[58]

6. *The Regrettable Ignorance of U.S. Legal Operators Concerning Natural Law*

Currently, ignorance and indifference best describe the historical mainstream attitude of American legal operators toward natural law. For example, an aspirant to the U.S. Supreme Court famously stated during her confirmation hearing in 2010: "I don't have a view of what are natural rights independent of the Constitution".[59] Deplorably, this view represents "the mainstream of contemporary [U.S.] legal thinking".[60]

This aspirant to U.S. Supreme Court justice's remarks were probably made without knowing the astonishing reflection by the German jurist Rudolf von Jhering in the 19th century in that, "he would probably not have written his work, *Der Zweck im Recht* had he been acquainted with the philosophy of the past, in particular with that of St. Thomas Aquinas".[61]

This ignorance is an unjustified departure from the founding principles of U.S. constitutional law. In effect, as Professor Hadley Arkes has demonstrated,[62] the protection of the 'natural rights' triad included in the Declaration of Independence (Life, Liberty, and the pursuit of Happiness) is the "whole purpose of government".[63] The Founding Fathers obtained that language, precisely, from the leftovers of traditional natural law that the 'natural rights' theory had left untouched.

---

[57] *See* Matthew S. Holland, "To Close the Circle of Our Felicities": *Caritas* and Jefferson's First Inaugural," *in* the Review of Politics, Vol. 66, No. 2 (Cambridge University Press, Spring 2004), pp. 181-205.

[58] Holland, *supra note* 572, at 94.

[59] O'Scannlain, supra *note* 2, at 1514 (referring to the Senate Committee on the Judiciary Holds a Hearing on the Elena Kagan Nomination).

[60] *Id.* at 1514.

[61] Rommen, *supra note* 10, at 120.

[62] Hadley Arkes, *Constitutional Illusions and Anchoring Truths: The Touchstone of the Natural Law* 8 (2010) (cited in O'Scannlain, supra note 2, at 1516).

[63] U.S. Declaration of Independence.

CHAPTER VIII:

SEARCHING FOR AN ACCEPTABLE STANDARD OF NATURAL LAW TO INTERPRET U.S. LAW

1. *In General*

Traditional natural law shaped the very essence of common law in England before the Reformation of the sixteenth century. British ecclesiastical courts applied canon law, and canon law is "imbued with the idea of natural law".[1] Jurists such as Henry de Bracton (d. 1268), Sir John Fortescue (d. cir. 1476), and Sir Edward Coke (d. cir. 1552) based their philosophical and practical legal scholarship on the basis of traditional natural law.[2]

Even until this day and contrary to what happened with the Anglo-Saxon common law after the Reformation, the civil law world maintained the codification of traditional natural law principles.[3] In effect, civil law codes are plagued with references to natural law principles such as, for example, "good faith and good morals,"[4] "principles of natural equity,"[5] or simply "equity".[6]

Despite the fact that the U.S. Constitution does not contain any explicit language referring to natural law and does not provide judges with any explicit standards to void positive law,[7] "formal natural-law thinking has never disappeared among judges"[8] in the United States. In fact, two her-

---

[1] Rommen, *supra note* 10, at 114.

[2] *Id.*

[3] *Id.* at 138 ("[a]longside the positive law stands yet another law which often exactly resembles the old natural law").

[4] *Id.* at 132.

[5] *Id.* at 138.

[6] Figueroa, *supra note* 101, Chapter IV(D).

[7] Baur, supra *note* 106, at 1537.

[8] Rommen, *supra note* 10, at 42.

meneutic methods concerning the use of natural law in jurisprudence have been offered as a criterion for determining the legitimacy of positive law- "standard legal positivism," and the "'aggressive' natural law jurisprudence".[9]

Standard legal positivism fully rejects any natural law strings to positive law. Rather, it proposes that there are no virtual or real links between morality and legislation,[10] and judges must apply exclusively the written law presented to them in a given case. On the other hand, the so-called "aggressive" natural law approach explains that judges must determine *motu proprio* the moral rules guiding their judgment to determine the legitimacy of legislation. The further argument is that "natural law moral principles are built into –or embedded within– American positive law itself,"[11] starting with the Constitution.

The dilemma of which theory to accept centers on the highly contentious questions of whether: (a) the Constitution and the Framers were aware of the existence of traditional natural law doctrine and the 'natural rights' theory; and (b) in the affirmative, what theory or principles did they decide to utilize to write the U.S. Constitution?[12]

This discussion must not be confused with the related, though different, determination of whether the use of natural law or natural rights principles to interpret the U.S. Constitution and legislation is desirable in today's U.S. society. In other words, what must be avoided is the intellectual dishonesty of rejecting the use of natural law elements for the interpretation of the U.S. Constitution. There should be no denying the fact that the Framers *did* consider natural law elements in the formation of the U.S. constitutional framework.

Experience shows that in the United States the power of judicial review first "examines whether the act is reasonable [or] arbitrary".[13] Eventually, a determination of reasonableness or justice is a determination founded on natural law. In practice, U.S. judges have approached their judicial review

---

[9]   Baur, supra note 106, at 1529.

[10]   Rommen, supra note 10, at 203 (alluding to the disregard of the traditional natural law principle, according to which "[m]orality calls [first] for fidelity to the laws of biology").

[11]   Baur, supra note 106, at 1530.

[12]   O'Scannlain, supra note 2, at 1514.

[13]   Rommen, supra note 10, at 198.

task not from an abstract perspective as the 'natural rights' theory would advise, but rather based on experience and tradition.[14]

2. *U.S. Jurisprudence Has Made Use of the Natural Law Concepts*

In its 1905 *Lochner v. New York* decision,[15] the U.S. Supreme Court incurred in what the anti-natural law establishment considered "natural law reasoning". The *Lochner* precedent was "corrected" sixty years later[16] when "all nine of the Justices [of the Supreme Court] ... decried the use of the natural law in judging".[17]

For example, in its 2008 *District of Columbia v. Heller* decision, the U.S. Supreme Court based its opinion, in part, in the alleged "natural right" to bear arms.[18] Beyond the holding of the case, the reasoning of the Court was defective in that it adhered to the long-standing Protestant paradigmatic view of natural law as a "subjective" perception according to which each judge may determine at will the content of natural law in a given case. This "subjective" approach to natural law disregards the actual nature of natural law as an objective discipline that may be perceived by human reason and understanding. Hence, the real dilemma of U.S. law is to shake itself off its feeble Protestant roots based on subjectivism and to find universal objective and rational natural law foundations to the most crucible constitutional dilemmas affecting the realm.

The current status of natural law in the U.S. has been clearly explained as follows:

natural law [is] under attack from both sides. To the left, it is an invention of mystics and religious conservatives. To the right, it is a dangerous invitation for judges to impose their own sense of justice on the country.[19]

---

[14] *Id.* at 228 "[o]ne should not wish to construct a system of natural law by methods proper to geometry; one must, on the contrary, continually consult experience and comparative law").

[15] Lochner v. New York, 198 U.S. 45 (1905).

[16] Griswold v. Connecticut, 381 U.S. 479 (1965).

[17] O'Scannlain, supra *note* 2, at 1515.

[18] 128 S.Ct. 2783 (2008),.

[19] O'Scannlain, supra *note* 2, at 1515.

3. *On the Natural Law Principles that Should Guide the Search for Natural Law in the United States*

In 2008, Pope Benedict XVI expressed that "natural law underlies the U.N.'s Universal Declaration of Human Rights".[20] Thus, to argue that human rights find their source of legitimacy and juridical force in positive law constitutes a historical inaccuracy that hurts the legal soul of the Western world. In turn, the human rights recognized and guaranteed by the U.S. Constitution derive, precisely, from natural law and exist independently of the government.[21] In fact,

> The Christian philosophy of law can demand this because in its eyes the nature of the state is not exhausted in the legal order, although the state must be essentially a constitutional state: it must be in the law. But the state is more than that, for it does not live by law alone.[22]

A. *A Correct Understanding of Human Nature*

It has been rightly stated that, "the establishment of the natural law further depends upon the doctrine of man's nature".[23] Despite the relevance of this topic, or instead because of it, we refer its treatment according to the doctrine of traditional natural law as reviewed on Chapter I: General Overview of Natural Law.

B. *Positive Law is a Part of the Juridical Pyramid, Not its Foundation*

Against the backdrop of positivism, traditional natural law has long proposed that positive law is not the ultimate foundation of legality.[24] Positive law is inseparable from morality[25] and from the philosophy of law.[26]

---

[20]   *Id.* at 1526, FN 74 (citing Pope Benedict XVI, Remarks to the United Nations General Assembly (Apr. 18, 2008), available at http://www.nytimes.com/2008/04/19/nyregion/18popeatun.html).

[21]   *Id.* at 1527.

[22]   Rommen, supra note 10, at 200.

[23]   *Id.* at 161.

[24]   *Id.* at 150 "[T]here are still other sources of law besides the positive will of the legislator").

[25]   *Id.* at 212 ("law and morality are not separated").

[26]   *Id.* at 188 ("[T]he philosophy of law cannot be detached from ethics").

The use of legal positivism made by totalitarianisms during the twentieth century demonstrates that "all law requires a moral foundation".[27] The positive legislator may enact as law "only what is moral".[28] In this sense, morality possesses a juridical ranking higher than positive law,[29] and hence no positive law is just outside of the moral law.[30]

Unlike the 'natural rights' theory, traditional natural law teaches that there exist three orders of obligations: "toward God, toward one's self, and toward one's fellow man".[31] Furthermore, there must be a healthy interaction between "internal morality and external legality"[32] according to traditional natural law. The internal morality is an element valuable not only in international law, but also in domestic and private law. For example, to determine intent in criminal matters, or the good faith of the parties in contractual matters (fraud), or the level of due care in tort law.[33]

Traditional natural law also recognizes that the human person may never be a means to another goal –either individual or collective– but it is always the "subject of right".[34] Again, contrary to the 'natural rights' theory, traditional natural law provided the legal reason to overcome slavery, which was "one of the most important achievements in the history of culture".[35]

Another example evidencing that positive law may never be the final foundation of itself resides in the field of contractual law where the law providing that agreements must be kept finds its foundation in the natural law principle of "truthfulness of speech".[36] Yet another instance is seen in

---

[27]   *Id.* at 213.

[28]   *Id.*

[29]   *Id.* at 202.

[30]   *Id.* at 190 ("[T]he legitimation of all law must ultimately be a moral one.").

[31]   *Id.* at 203.

[32]   *Id.* at 205 and 206 ("[E]thics embraces the total activity of man, his inner and outward acts. Acts of obedience toward parents, of truthful speech, and of fidelity to one's given word certainly do not lose their moral character merely because through their externalization they become legal acts").

[33]   *Id.* at 205.

[34]   *Id.* at 207.

[35]   *Id.*

[36]   *Id.* at 225.

that the latter provides the argument for restricting "the unruly vital forces that plague man ... in order that man can really live as man".[37]

As a result, positive law accords to justice only and exclusively when it is based on the ethical principles taught by traditional natural law. As an author has rightly stated,

> When little or no respect any longer exists for any authority; when marriage generally ceases to be differentiated from concubinage and promiscuity; when the honor of one's fellow citizen is no longer respected and oaths no longer have force, then the possibility of social living, of order in human affairs, vanishes altogether.[38]

C. *On the Interaction between Man, Religion, and the State*

Man is by his constitution a religious animal.[39] Justice and mercy are substantial parts of religion. When these ethical values are expressed in their correct substance and form, they become the basis of civil society.[40] As a result, atheism is not only against reason but also contrary to human instincts.[41] Edmund Burke clarified the traditional natural view on the inhumanity of atheism:

> [t]he most horrid and cruel blow, that can be offered to civil society, is through atheism ... the infidels, are outlaws of the constitution; not of this country [England], but of the human race. They are never, never to be supported, never to be tolerated.[42]

Contemporary reality shows that if traditional natural law is not the decisive foundation of enacted laws, positive law emerges as a threat to man himself. This reality is patently perceivable in the areas of human life and marriage where unbelievably strong forces threaten the roots of the Christian convictions that have shaped the Western legal culture.

---

[37] *Id.* at 212.

[38] *Id.* at 257.

[39] Burke, *supra note* 17, at 88.

[40] *Id.* at 87.

[41] *Id.* at 88.

[42] Edmund Burke, *Speech on the Second Reading of a Bill for the Relief of Protestant Dissenters* (1773), *in* Rogers, *supra note* 18, at 575 ("of all men, the most dangerous is a warm, hot-headed, zealous atheist").

D. *Traditional Natural Law is the True Foundation of Government*

The rights of man –which are given to him by the Creator in accordance to nature– exist in total independence of the government.[43] In this sense, the government is a "contrivance of human wisdom to provide for human wants".[44] The rights the Creator bestowed on man, such as life, property, and the pursuit of happiness,[45] belong to all the creatures. Hence, when government acts against of, or fails to protect, the rights that natural law has given to man, it becomes tyranny, whether monarchical or democratic, or republican or whatever its denomination may be.[46]

This is not to say that traditional natural law sanctions a political regimen in particular.[47] What traditional natural law teaches is that any form of government which does not "recognize the fundamental rights of the person and of the family is tyrannical and may, therefore, rightly be resisted".[48]

E. *The Democratic Ideal Needs a Moral Foundation*

Aristotle had already recognized that democracy has many striking points of resemblance with tyranny.[49] As Edmund Burke sustained, "in a democracy the majority of the citizens is capable of exercising the most cruel oppressions upon the minority".[50] With genuine clairvoyance he also recognized the fallen nature of man when he stated that,

---

[43]   Burke, supra note 17, at 57.

[44]   *Id.*

[45]   *Id.* at 104.

[46]   Rommen, supra note 10, at 259 ("St. Thomas holds that the constitution must be suited to the character of the people and to its moral vigor").

[47]   *Id.* at 265 ("neither the capitalistic nor the feudal system of property is imposed by the natural law"). Id., at 219 ("[b]y natural law, for example, more than one form of state or government is legitimate").

[48]   *Id.*

[49]   Edmund Burke, Speech on the Acts of Uniformity (1772), in Rogers, supra note 18, at 468 (stating "[t]o take away from men their lives, their liberty, or their property, those things, for the protection of which society was introduced, is great hardship and intolerable tyranny.").

[50]   Burke, supra note 17, at 122.

[h]istory consists for the greater part of the miseries brought upon the world by pride, ambition, avarice, revenge, lust, sedition, hypocrisy, ungoverned zeal, and all the train of disorderly appetites which shake the public with the same.[51]

Burke also affirms that these vices are the causes of political unrests, but that, ultimately, "religion, morals, laws, prerogatives, privileges, liberties, rights of men are –just– the pretexts" behind those vices.[52]

Ultimately, only a political regime that finds its moral *substratum* in the traditional natural law and derives its legitimacy from beyond transient majorities and enlightened governments is more humane and, therefore, destined to last.

F. *Government Positions are Held in Trust of the People*

The concept of trust has a clear legal connotation in both civil and common law systems. In civil law it is the concept of the *fiduciario*, that is, of he who acts on behalf and in representation of another in a position of confidence. In common law systems, the trustee is a fundamental institution of private, commercial, financial, and business law in general without which the whole legal system would just not function. The concept of *fides* or confidence, trust, is also at the center of this institution.[53] Accordingly, the idea that those in government positions act as "trustees" of the people means that they are also to "account for their conduct in that trust to"[54] the Creator. In that sense, it does not seem possible to truly follow moral virtue in politics without the inexcusable guidance of true religion. Otherwise, all temporary good intentions become "the lust of selfish will".[55]

It becomes logical, hence, that the government must care for all the citizens without difference, by acting and correcting where it must, and by

---

[51]   *Id.* at 137.

[52]   *Id.*

[53]   Article, Is the Lack of Trusts an Impediment for Expanding Business Opportunities in Latin America? 24 Ariz. J. Int'l & Comp. L. 701 (2007). For a review of civil and common law trusts, see generally Dante Figueroa, Civil Law Trusts: Is the Lack of Trusts an Impediment for Expanding Business Opportunities in Latin America? 24 Ariz. J. Int'l & Comp. L. 701 (2007).

[54]   Burke, *supra note* 17, at 90.

[55]   *Id.* at 91.

refraining from acting where it should.[56] Private virtue and wisdom cannot be separated from public virtue.[57]

A testimony on the solidity of these traditional natural law principles comes from Cicero, who in his day urged his fellow citizens:

> To follow the path of justice and moderation ... to resist the temptations of their passions and to fulfill their duties to the best of their abilities [and to serve] as an example for imitation [seeking] to benefit the state and its citizens rather than himself.[58]

G. *Justice May Only Be Obtained According t o Traditional Natural Law*

Cicero recognized the intimate link between natural law and justice for the exercise of force in society when he asserted that,

> [j]ustice consists of those laws of nature that apply to human beings. Justice is the foundation of every society and the most essential element of human relationships. Because justice issues from natural law, all forms of justice in their essence are matters of nature, not human convention. Human convention can strengthen the application of natural justice in a state by means of custom and usage.[59]

Cicero also explained that certain "conceptions and practices of justice become over time customary by virtue of the advantages they yield to those who discover and learn them".[60] In that sense, he rejected the teachings of some who taught that "the specifics of law as if it had nothing to do with justice".[61]

In sum, Cicero's views —which were not changed by traditional natural law— clearly contradict the conception advanced by the 'natural rights' theory that justice is simply a matter of human convention based on agreement.[62]

---

[56]   *Id.* at 184.

[57]   *Id.* at 47-48.

[58]   Poulakos, supra note 77, at 162.

[59]   *Id.* at 159.

[60]   *Id.*

[61]   *Id.*

[62]   *Id.*

H. *The Twin Traditional Natural Law Principles of Subsidiarity and Solidarity Must Guide Government Action*

Much could be said about these two remarkable principles first enunciated by Pope Leo XIII in his Encyclical Letter *Rerum Novarum* of 1891. At their essence these no principles state that under no circumstances can the human person be sacrificed for the sake of the community. And this is the whole meaning, purpose, and goal of government according to traditional natural law.

CHAPTER IX:

THE PRESSING DILEMMAS OF WHO ENFORCES NATURAL LAW, AND UNDER WHAT PRINCIPLES AND RULES

Natural law thinking has not stopped-even in this era of entrenched skepticism or outright antagonism toward traditional natural law in the Western legal world. Amongst those who strive to revitalize traditional natural law and to bring it closer to the applicators of the positive law, two questions are ever present: first, the dilemma of who enforces natural law rules; and second, what are the principles and rules that traditional natural law proposes.

1. The Contentious Issue of Who has the Authority to Determine and Enforce Natural Law Once the Existence of Natural Law Has Been Accepted

An American judge has acutely stated that,

[e]ven the jurists who are well-known for believing in the natural law, Justice Clarence Thomas and Judges Robert Bork and William Pryor, for instance, do not believe that judges have the authority to enforce it.[1]

In the constitutional paradigm of democratic government that arose from the French Revolution,[2] the task of enforcing the natural law would fall onto one or more of the branches of government. The most-well known approaches to the question of what branch of government is the

---

[1]   O'Scannlain, supra *note* 2, at 1519, Fn. 43.

[2]   Gentz, supra *note* 19, at 53 ("[T]he French Revolution ... began by a violation of rights, every step of its progress was a violation of rights ... until it had succeeded to establish absolute wrong").

most appropriate to enforce the natural law antagonize on whether this task corresponds to the judiciary: one affirms it while the other denies it.[3]

In truth, the attribution of the power to determine the content of natural law to judges sets them "not only above the lawmaker but in theory even above the framers of constitutional law".[4] To the contemporary legal mind this premise is utterly unacceptable. On the other hand, in practice in the U.S. separation of powers model, judges *do* create law, and "still appeal . . . to the natural law or natural justice.[5] Otherwise, how would it be possible to explain the judicial invalidation power over positive law that is "at variance with the natural law?"[6] Only an appeal to a law superior than positive law explains such invalidation powers.

2. *The Question of What Hermeneutical Principles and Rules Should be Used to Determine and Apply Natural Law*

A number of alternatives exist concerning the question of which are the guiding principles for interpreting natural law based on the Constitution; namely: the rule centering on the literal text of the Constitution; the axiom focusing on the meaning of the constitutional provisions; and lastly, the rule prioritizing the historicity of the Constitution.

Whatever the hermeneutical rule adopted, reality demonstrates that the role of constitutional law is not to reinvent a society, but to perfect it. Certain natural law principles lay at the heart of Western constitutional law, whose common features are as follows:

(a) Natural law principles are God-given and immutable at both the individual and collective levels. They may not be amended or impinged by constitutional provisions;

(b) Natural law principles are prior and superior to the government;

(c) Natural law principles should not be used to twist, or re-shape institutions that are connatural to the human person;

---

[3]   Robert Bork, *The Tempting of America: the Political Seduction of the Law* 66 (1990), cited in O'Scannlain, supra *note* 2, at 1521 (stating "I am far from denying that there is a natural law, but I do deny [that] judges have any greater access to that law than do the rest of us").

[4]   Rommen, *supra note* 10, at 248-9.

[5]   *Id.* at 260-1.

[6]   *Id.* at 261-2.

(d) Natural law principles reject the idea of a supposed abstract 'state of nature' according to which men were good to one another before civil society corrupted him;

(e) Natural law principles present the subsidiariety rule as key for the political, economical, and social organization of society;

f) Natural law principles explain that organized society has deputized to the State the power to rule over men, but all power ultimately emanates from the Creator in a position of trust;

(g) Natural law principles command political communities to refrain from using paradigms proven to be philosophically bankrupt, such as the 'natural rights' theory;

(h) Natural law principles explain that all political societies demonstrate that traditions are at the heart of their very foundation; and

(i) Natural law principles call for a correct understanding of human nature, far from the Hobbian irremediably pessimistic notion, or the sentimentalist/romantic view of the Sophists, Locke, and Rousseau. Instead, traditional natural law teaches that –alongside the goodness of human nature– the political order must be "aware of the demonic element in man's nature,"[7] which requires constant constraint and also "a positive, earthly sanction".[8]

3. *Proposition of the Real Natural Rights of Man*

In Edmund Burke's words, according to the traditional natural law "the protection of man's life, liberty, and property, constitute his most fundamental rights as man".[9] These rights may reach its concrete realization in civil society alone.[10] Besides these fundamental rights, traditional natural law recognizes other "derivative rights of man in civil society,"[11] which include:

the right to justice under the law, the right of all men to the fruits of their industry, the right to the means of making their industry fruitful, the right to the ac-

---

[7]   *Id.* at 254.

[8]   *Id.* at 253.

[9]   Stanlis, supra note 296, at 76.

[10]   *Id.*

[11]   *Id.* at 77.

quisitions of their parents, the right to the nourishment and improvement of their offspring, the right to instruction in life, and to consolation in death.[12]

The reason why traditional natural law insists in affirming that the institution of private property is of natural law is that without it, "in the long run man cannot exist, cannot make good his right to marriage or to a family or to security of life, and cannot maintain his sphere of individual right to a life of his own".[13]

In definitive, such is the vitality of property for human development that "whoever has no property all too easily becomes property".[14]

4. *A Correct Understanding of Democratic Legitimacy*

A fundamental dogma of the French Revolution was that of the popular sovereignty theory. According to this axiom, the general will of the people is the sole legitimate criterion for government.[15] Traditional natural law, instead –as Edmund Burke explained– held that the popular will "is not the final test of conscience for legislators, nor the ultimate moral basis of government".[16]

Beyond popular will, traditional natural law appeals to the eternal, immutable law[17] as a guarantee against the arbitrary claims emanating from popular sovereignty. A "true constitutional democracy"[18] is one where the people shall not be made to do what it is not just or correct. Unlike traditional natural law, the 'natural rights' theory promoted the principle of unrestrained popular despotism, or what Edmund Burke called "Jacobin democracy".[19] In fact, Burke condemned Jacobinism as it warped the "true democratic principle that every man's free will shall be as unfettered as possible [to] mean that the free will of the collective people shall be fettered in nothing".[20]

---

[12]   *Id.*

[13]   Rommen, *supra note* 10, at 233.

[14]   *Id.* at 234.

[15]   See generally, Figueroa, supra note 101.

[16]   Stanlis, *supra note* 296, at 239.

[17]   *Id.* at 74.

[18]   *Id.* at 244.

[19]   *Id.*

[20]   *Id.*

To the "Jacobin or Rousseauist heresy of *vox populi vox dei,*"[21] Edmund Burke argued for "a civil order founded upon constitutional law and the Natural Law".[22] In this system, he argued, "majorities and minorities, corporate groups and individuals, rulers and ruled alike, all are *sub Deo et sub lege*".[23] In this order, the power of the political sovereign (either monarchical or democratic) "could never be the ultimate source of law, because law itself made the political sovereign".[24] Furthermore, in Burke's view, representing the traditional natural law, "government is an instrument given to man by God [and] all human affairs [are] also subject to God's reason and will".[25]

In consequence, political sovereignty and the Constitution itself find their ultimate *moral* basis on the natural law,[26] that is, into the law given to man by God.

5. The Foundations of a Free State of Law according to Traditional Natural Law[27]

Traditional natural law was built as a philosophical science over the course of many centuries before the beginning of a systematic distortion campaign with the Reformation in the 16th century. However, as it has been repeatedly stated in this study, the soundness of traditional natural law principles has not been deafened by the overwhelming omnipresent noise of the 'natural rights' theory.

In fact, several of the key traditional natural law principles still resonate more than ever for the honest intellectual in the Western legal system. Those traditional natural law rules include the following:

(a) Religion is the ultimate foundation of ethics in politics and of legal systems.[28]

(b) God created man and bestowed on him inviolable rights.[29]

---

[21] *Id.* at 245.

[22] *Id.*

[23] *Id.*

[24] *Id.*

[25] *Id.*

[26] *Id.*

[27] Reichstag Speech, *supra note* 30.

[28] *Id.* ("systems of law have almost always been based on religion.").

(c) Man does not create himself but "has a nature that he must respect and that he cannot manipulate at will".[30] Pope Benedict XVI has explained this circumstance more thoroughly:

> He [man] is intellect and will, but he is also nature, and his will is rightly ordered if he listens to his nature, respects it and accepts himself for who he is, as one who did not create himself. In this way, and in no other, is true human freedom fulfilled.[31]

(d) Politics is legitimate so long as it conforms to justice.[32] Indeed, justice is the foundation of government.[33] Power may not be divorced from what is right.[34]

(e) Christianity has never proposed a particular political regime, but has identified natural law and reason as the key elements of any authentically human political system.[35]

(f) The majority principle is insufficient to protect the most essential dignity of the human person.[36]

---

[29] *Id.* ("there is a Creator God is what gave rise to the idea of human rights, the idea of the equality of all people before the law, the recognition of the inviolability of human dignity in every single person and the awareness of people's responsibility for their actions").

[30] *Id.*

[31] *Id.*

[32] *Id.* (political "success is subordinated to the criterion of justice, to the will to do what is right, and to the understanding of what is right.").

[33] *Id.* ("[w]ithout justice – what else is the State but a great band of robbers?", as Saint Augustine once said").

[34] *Id.* ("[w]e [Germans] have seen how power became divorced from right, how power opposed right and crushed it, so that the State became an instrument for destroying right – a highly organized band of robbers, capable of threatening the whole world and driving it to the edge of the abyss").

[35] *Id.* ("[U]nlike other great religions, Christianity has never proposed a revealed body of law to the State and to society, that is to say a juridical order derived from revelation. Instead, it has pointed to nature and reason as the true sources of law.").

[36] *Id.* ("for the fundamental issues of law, in which the dignity of man and of humanity is at stake, the majority principle is not enough").

CONCLUSION

The concept of traditional natural law lies at the heart of the division be-tween Catholic doctrine[1] and Protestantism, which –in a nutshell– is the elaboration of a partial and selective denial of the wholesomeness of Catholic doctrine. The first and foremost error of Protestantism is the denial of the principle of separation of Church and State. The erection of the political head of a *polis* (British King) as the supreme pastor for the salvation of souls has, since the Reformation, raised the natural skepticism of superior and honest minds. Five hundred years later, that skepticism has evolved in what is the logical fruit of the reformation experiment-widespread unbelief.[2]

The 'natural rights' theory is a result of political Protestantism. This work has striven to identify the many errors of that theory; amongst them, the key and pernicious mistake of separation between politics and morality, both in private and public.[3] Another demonstration of this error is the positivist split between law and morality, which denies the evidence that "in the human soul lies the ineradicable demand that the law must live in morality".[4]

---

[1] *Id.* ("[T]he idea of natural law is today viewed as a specifically Catholic doctrine").

[2] Barker, *supra note* 771, at 129-130, stating that:

"In juridical circles, the Natural Law has been under attack for more than a century, not just in the United States, but throughout the Western World. Those attacks have made it easier for activist courts and weak or misguided legislators and administrators to reject or ignore the Natural Law foundations of Western Civilization and of the United States Constitution, and to adopt programs that deny the inherent dignity and essential equality of every human being, that weaken the family, and distort education, that seek to make all groups and organizations in society subservient to the state, and that even deny legal protection to the weakest and most innocent among us".

[3] Rommen, *supra note* 10, at 265 ("[P]olitics is and remains a part of the moral universe. For it is inexcusable to view politics merely as the technique or art of achieving and retaining social power for some selfish end through the skillful exploitation of human weaknesses, by deceit or by terrorist methods").

[4] *Id.* at 266.

In addition, the 'natural rights' theory has so watered down traditional natural law in that it has denied the double conservative/revolutionary essence of that discipline.[5] In effect, on the one hand, traditional natural law is the main defender of tradition, stability, and the progress of humanity. On the other, traditional natural law provides the most stellar justification for insurrection against arbitrary acts from the political authority since it "alone can we solve the crucial political problem of the legitimacy of power and the duty of free persons to obey".[6]

Conclusively, the Western legal tradition emerged from "the encounter between Jerusalem, Athens and Rome–from the encounter between Israel's monotheism, the philosophical reason of the Greeks and Roman law [and] this three-way encounter has shaped the inner identity of Europe".[7] When this identity is denied as a result of the rejection of traditional natural law, the end result is that the Western culture "is left in a state of culturelessness and at the same time extremist and radical movements emerge to fill the vacuum,"[8] where force prevails over law.

---

[5] *Id.* at 262 (what is called "the old distinction between unlawful sedition and justifiable resistance to the power of the state").

[6] *Id.* at 266.

[7] Reichstag Speech, *supra note* 30.

[8] *Id.*

CHAPTER V:
A CONCEPTUAL REVIEW OF THE SYSTEMATIC DISTORTION OF TRADITIONAL NATURAL LAW AND ITS SUBSTITUTION BY THE "NATURAL RIGHTS" THEORY

CHAPTER VI

THE INROADS OF THE 'NATURAL RIGHTS'
THEORY INTO THE FOUNDING DOCUMENTS OF
THE UNITED STATES OF AMERICA 107

CHAPTER VII
SEARCHING FOR THE NATURAL LAW NOTIONS THAT INSPIRED THE FOUNDING FATHERS

CHAPTER VIII
SEARCHING FOR AN ACCEPTABLE STANDARD OF NATURAL LAW TO INTERPRET U.S. LAW

CHAPTER IX

THE PRESSING DILEMMAS OF WHO ENFORCES NATURAL LAW, AND UNDER WHAT PRINCIPLES AND RULES